Angel
IN BLACK

Angel
IN BLACK

A Musical Life in Letters, 1925–1973

Beverly Shaffer Gast

Order this book online at www.trafford.com
or email orders@trafford.com

Most Trafford titles are also available at major online book retailers.

Printed in the United States of America.

ISBN: 978-1-4269-7485-4 (sc)
ISBN: 978-1-4669-0031-8 (e)

Library of Congress Control Number: 2011960894

Trafford rev. 11/17/2011

 www.trafford.com

North America & international
toll-free: 1 888 232 4444 (USA & Canada)
phone: 250 383 6864 ♦ fax: 812 355 4082

Dedication

To my grandchildren:

Traci Jeanne
Ashley Grace
G. Travis
Andrew Karl
Alexandra Beverly
Emily Sidney
William Aaron

Contents

Acknowledgments

Tales of my sister Elaine's musical career and her amazing achievements seemed to bring a physical response. Often, whenever they were told, the sensation of a chill was mentioned. These comments convinced me the story would be written.

My siblings, Robert W. Shaffer (Carol) and Patricia A. Shaffer, knew the vast collection of materials we held and encouraged the project. My adult children, Gregory (Nancy), Lisa Pfeil (Fred), and Brian (Tricia) cherished the story of "Aunt Elaine" for generations to come.

John Solum, musician friend of Elaine's and faithful correspondent to our family, read the manuscript and encouraged my progress. Cyanne Gresham also read and gave me valuable heartfelt comments.

Merrill Furman, a writer who served as editor in the earlier chapters and became engrossed in its historic appeal, happening at a time when women were denied equal opportunities. I credit her for the title: Angel in Black.

Joan and Robbie Robinson of Boise, Idaho, faithful friends and published authors, urged me to complete my work and even passed its theme to a young screenwriter. A Hollywood producer received the "treatment," wary of its success since it lacked any inkling of scandal.

Here I acknowledge Lynn Lewis, the exceedingly helpful person who entered the project as an angel. She recognized my frustration with extensive manuscript formatting and freely offered her expertise in sensitive, technical formatting. I am deeply indebted to Lynn for her timely, generous involvement and friendship. I can say, "we" finished the book!

Thank you to fellow residents at The Hill at Whitemarsh who kept me accountable.

Prologue

This is the story of Elaine Shaffer, the trailblazing musician who became the first female concert flutist in the world. At a time when opportunities were closed to women and orchestral venues boasted signs, "Only Men Need Apply," Elaine's extraordinary talent and perseverance forged a career that led her to soaring heights. Self-taught until her years at the prestigious Curtis Institute of Music in Philadelphia, Elaine grew in musical stature under the tutelage of the renowned William Kincaid, principal flute of the Philadelphia Orchestra. *Newsweek* (Dec. 1962) wrote, "Miss Shaffer is known from Munich to Melbourne as queen of her instrument." Accolades followed, year after year, country after country, with Elaine exceeding even her own standards of excellence.

Her life, short in years, indeed exemplified a rare intensity. As her sister, I have chronicled an ambitious concert career through twenty years of voluminous letters, diary entries, newspaper critics' reviews, photographs and my own memories. One incredible chapter followed another, from her scholarship to the Curtis Institute of Music, to performances with more than thirty major world orchestras.

A musical future with international fame was not unusual for a child prodigy, but exceptional for an adolescent searching for her own teacher. In our Depression era home, our parents had scarce opportunity to offer formal music lessons to the eldest.

The Curtis Institute of Music opened the door to the symphonic world for Elaine. During a summer season with the Robin Hood Dell Orchestra she played under the baton of Maestro Dimitri Mitropolous. She attended rehearsals with the Philadelphia Orchestra under Maestro Eugene Ormandy after she was appointed associate flute. A few years later, she was principal flute with the summer Hollywood Bowl Symphony, again under Ormandy. Her first full employment came with a call to join the Kansas City Philharmonic, followed by the Houston Symphony, both under Maestro Efrem Kurtz whom she would one day wed.

After five years with the Houston Symphony, buoyed by audience response and critiques, Elaine launched a solo career in Europe. Impeccable musicianship and travel between countries and continents found her in the company of royalty and other luminaries—Herman Hesse, Sir Jacob Epstein, Karl Barth, Marc Chagall, John Kenneth Galbraith, Pablo Casals, Andres Segovia and Yehudi Menuhin. At the Engadine Festival in St. Moritz, Switzerland, Herman Hesse said, "You played as a daughter of Handel or Mozart." Ernest Bloch dedicated two compositions to her and wrote, "You have passed the conservatory of God."

Elaine's artistry and humanity combined naturally with a distinct spiritual nature reflected in the depth of her musical interpretation. "If the music talks," she once said, "then each individual in the audience is obliterated into a collective subconscious, taken out of his everyday life and given a glimpse of the unseen, of eternity." Adoring audiences responded with deep emotion and compared her performances to those of classical guitarist Andres Segovia and to famous harpist Nicanor Zabaleta, with whom she often performed. Success followed success.

After the diagnosis of a fatal illness, Elaine set for herself an unimaginable goal—to undertake, from memory, six Bach Flute Sonatas. A colossal task, even for anyone in robust health, that performance became her greatest triumph.

The Bach Sonata concert in London in Oct. 1972 may have been a likely theme when *Time* magazine interviewed her for the music page of their "Man of the Year" issue (Jan.1973). Instead, under the title Queen of the Flute, it featured her association with Aaron Copland and his *Duo for Flute and Piano*, commissioned in honor of William Kincaid, her beloved teacher. She performed the premier and later the recording of Copland's work. *Time* wrote, "Her solo career as a flutist was a virtual impossibility in the U.S. She was not just queen of the flute, but one of the 2 or 3 finest flutists, male or female."

The musical world was calling until the stunning announcement of her death from lung cancer in London's Middlesex Hospital on February 19, 1973. Her premature passing came at the height of dazzling world recognition.

I found myself physically and emotionally in many facets of this story. Countless personal letters prompted my obsession to recreate her unwavering determination which unfolded an "impossible dream." She is, as Thoreau said after the death of John Brown, "more alive than ever [she] was."

An Unlikely Beginning

The Altoona Silk Manufacturing Mill offered employment to school students like Catharine Marie Treese and Rex Winfield Shaffer before they completed their education. Schooling and a high school diploma seemed a luxury in both of their hard-working families. Both of these young people understood that priority in their households and in many of their generation. Rex and Catharine's paycheck helped support their families.

"The Mill" became the natural setting for friendship and romance despite the long tiring days tending the clanging machinery. On their feet for hours in the shop, still they enjoyed evenings at the local roadhouse dance hall, where they learned the latest dance steps to popular tunes. Vaudeville troupes with comic skits, acrobats and ragtime banjo bands brought entertainment to Altoona's Mischler Theater.

Rex and Catharine stood before the church pastor in the parsonage where their simple wedding was performed. They honeymooned with a trip to New York City and the Statue of Liberty. Catharine was nineteen years old. Their first child, a daughter, Elaine, arrived on October 22, 1925, Rex's 22nd birthday.

The responsible new father now looked to the Pennsylvania Railroad as a more promising workplace. Several generations of men and women on both sides of their families found a trade in "the shops," an industry that supported Altoona. Rex found the drudgery and routine, with grime, grit and coal dust, confined him to black, sweaty, greasy work clothes as he trudged Altoona's hills with his black metal lunch box. Still young, restless and ambitious, he opened himself to a more expansive way of life.

Rex learned of an opportunity to join a growing sales force. The possibility of more suitable work lured him away him away from the reliable PRR and before long he moved his family to the small town of Lock Haven. Catharine left friends and relatives behind but welcomed the new beginning. She settled into the red brick three-bedroom rental house, just a block from the Susquehanna River, while Rex explored his new sales territory.

Rex proved himself "a born salesman." For years he promoted his line of cookies and crackers for the Colonial (later Keebler) Biscuit Company. Week after week he drove his faithful Ford hundreds of miles to out-of-the-way customers scattered about the Central Pennsylvania countryside. His affable nature and good humor, combined with the quality of his product, usually led to orders. At the end of his day, Rex would head home to address a large, brown envelope to the head office, stuffed with the day's business, to drop at the post office. Though he worked hard and made sales, his salary and commission never seemed to expand beyond the essentials for a growing family.

Catharine's frugal management stretched the household's limited resources, juggling the bills each month. She dreaded the creditor's knock. Eventually, four children completed the family. Three born in Altoona entered the Robb Elementary School in Lock Haven within a few years of each other. First there was Elaine then I, Beverly, twenty months later in 1927. Robert, the only son, joined his sisters in 1930. Seven years later, while living in Lock Haven, a beautiful baby girl was born. Patricia Ann delighted us as we filled our summer days attending to her as mother's helpers. Each of us never lacked a generous share of our mother's loving attention.

One summer Rex, on a gambler's whim, took a 25¢ chance on a deluxe model automobile that sat on display for several weeks at the local fireman's street carnival. A bright red Packard Six fascinated him with its beauty and design. Ever since owning his first Model T Ford, he took an interest in the automobile industry. On the carnival's closing night, Lock Haven's townspeople turned out to hear who would win the prized car.

And the winning ticket goes to . . . Rex Shaffer!

Rex became a celebrity in his hometown. Catharine could only hope that their financial tide might turn with the sale of this "gift from God." However, Rex, enamored of the shiny new vehicle, could not bear to part with it. He drove it with pride, happy to offer rides to customers and friends. He beamed behind the wheel on Sunday drives with the family. No, the Packard would not go; instead he sold the Ford.

Our parents, that era in history, and a secure, confined way of life, all played a part in the formation of Elaine's personality. Entries in her childhood diary revealed her traits of self-discipline and dogged determination. Elaine maximized opportunities and surmounted limitations and obstacles. She emerged from this unlikely beginning to rise to unimaginable zeniths in the musical world. Asked whether her talent could be traced in our family history, Elaine replied, "Perhaps they did not have the opportunity." A modest response from a woman who made her *own* opportunity.

At the joyous celebration of Rex and Catherine's 50th wedding anniversary, I discovered a long-held family secret. Elaine was conceived before our parents' marriage ceremony at the parsonage. The news of an unexpected child had been received by them as a gift—not as an inconvenience or foolish mistake. Our mother thought Elaine and I had found the wedding license many years before, but had kept that information to ourselves. She recalled the day we rummaged through old documents. "You were much too quiet and didn't come promptly when I called you for dinner. You must have found the papers!" she said.

No, we never knew. Elaine, I believe, would have delighted in the story of her special birth.

Early School Days

Our life in Central Pennsylvania in the 1930's resembled that of others we knew. Lock Haven and Williamsport, our hometowns, sat along the banks of the wide, flowing Susquehanna River, shadowed by the blue-gray Allegheny Mountains. We settled for a world of home and neighborhood until we entered the public school's first grade. My older sister, Elaine, seemed to find all she needed there to feed her soul, exercise her body and stimulate her curiosity.

Each day's happenings noted in Elaine's small faux leather diary in mature Palmer Method handwriting carefully tracked each day's high and low temperature and the hour of bedtimes. The titles of Saturday movie matinees revealed our favorite screen idols: Shirley Temple, Jane Withers, Jackie Cooper, or Deanna Durbin. That simple diversion expanded our inner life and opened a world beyond our dreams.

Rugged, challenging sports and games appealed to Elaine. She joined the neighborhood boys in touch football, softball, horseshoes and marbles. Elaine loved a very special early-rising day to head off with Dad to a clear stream with her fishing rod. (It became a life-long delight whenever she discovered lakes or streams in far-off places.) Hours of ice skating on the frozen river or sledding on nearby hills were the best of fun during long cold winters. In early spring we ran with town folk to line the river bank to watch the ice jam break up; huge thick blocks of ice crashed together and edged their flow downstream.

Elaine and I were twenty months apart in age. Our names were mentioned as one—Elaine/Beverly—and social invitations included us both. Inseparable, we were never taken for twins, even with look-alike dresses and huge matching hair bows in complimentary colors. Our chestnut hair set off barber haircuts, "tips of the ears showing." Physically, Elaine was robust, sturdy, full of health. An expressive countenance with two remarkable dimples pleased admiring adults. As her sister, I was considered fragile, even sickly, with a thin frame. Elaine's appetite was hearty while I refused most foods, except for white bread and jelly. A double bed during school years accommodated us both. We passed any sickness to the other and a dose of castor oil kept us indoors and absent from school only a day.

Elaine had a characteristic sense of order and attention to detail. She arranged her side of the closet with a system foreign to me. I understood her irritation as I tossed whatever I chose on the nearest chair. The diary noted incessant cleaning of the house and "redding" its rooms on Saturdays. School assignments received excellent grades with their precise and artistic math charts and diagrams, colored world maps and prize-winning thrift posters.

We anticipated visits with grandmother Treese and her windup Victrola. We carefully positioned the needle over the RCA Victor Red Seal discs, lay on the floor, our ears close to the speakers. Stirring military marches were worn white with wear. We never tired of the dramatic tenor, John Charles Thomas, as he sang "The Holy City."

Elaine produced living room "concerts" to mimic radio's Major Bowes' Amateur Hour. Programs in pencil featured the small mouth organ, the ocarina, the kazoo, a toy xylophone and even the rhythmic clacking of "the bones," prepared by the local butcher. Sister acts, song duets, and tap dancing guaranteed an approving audience of family, visiting relatives and the pet fox terrier.

The simplicity of that little mouth organ prompted Elaine to ask our grandparents to help her shop at Winter's Music Store in Altoona. Her young age of eleven, obvious to the clerk, made him offer an instrument much like her own. "No," she said, "I want to see one that plays sharps and flats." She left the music store with a M. Hohner harmonica with a double reed. Her diary noted, "I sent away for a book of harmonica music, seventeen songs. I want to learn them all." Community and school programs soon included her playing the new harmonica.

Years when Elaine might have begun formal music lessons were already past. And then a school announcement excited her as if it were a personal gift. President Franklin Delano Roosevelt proposed an educational program in America's public schools, designed to revitalize the Depression economy. His WPA (Works Project Administration) provided for unemployed musicians to offer instrumental lessons at no cost in the public schools. Those students who owned a violin were chosen early.

Oct. 26, 1936 diary entry: *Mr. Kleckner came in to look at violins. I don't have any.*

In careful penmanship a plea to a favorite auntie was not fruitful.

> *Lock Haven, Pa*
> *October 14, 1936*
>
> *Dear Betty,*
>
> *How are you? In school they are going to teach violin lessons for free. I wonder if you would lend me yours if I get it fixed? Mother said if I make out alright Daddy is going to get me a new one. Mother is going to try to get Beverly one too. The man at the high school that teaches the band is going to teach 4, 5, and 6 grades. Answer soon.*
>
> *Lots of love,*
> *Elaine*

A school instrument soon materialized and a schedule of practice, lessons, and orchestra rehearsals filled each day. The wonderful world of music captivated her. She managed to learn the cello as well as the violin and even the timpani. One day, bereft of schoolmates: Oct. 13, 1937: *I went to band practice but it was marching.* None of her instruments had a place in the marching band. She longed to join the uniformed students playing spirited marches at Saturday football games.

An old cedar chest in the attic held unfamiliar treasures to explore. Elaine pulled away blankets and fabric pieces and felt something cold to her hand, a small black lead fife. Putting it to her lips she blew a shrill sound. The simple scale is what she asked of the five holes before taking it to the school's clarinet teacher. The little pipe had limited usefulness, he said, and then remembered a bulky black wooden flute in the band closet.

The intricacies of the new instrument consumed her time and interest with no break over the summer, until mother reminded her that she needed time off before school would begin again. Instead, Elaine continued to press the clarinet teacher to unlock all he knew of the flute's potential, even to help her learn double and triple tonguing.

District and state band and orchestra competitions were an incentive to match her capabilities with other young musicians in Pennsylvania. She consistently took first chair in the woodwind section. At one meet, assigned the second chair, she challenged the first chair player. Elaine came away as first flute.

Devotion to her instrument and her wide interest in music made her talents known as she performed in the community. She conducted the orchestra at Williamsport High School's Spring Concert in her senior year, a distinctive honor. At her graduation ceremonies in 1943, the program featured her as piccolo soloist.

Once she completed high school, Elaine's dire need to purchase her own instrument dominated her concerns. The band director in her former school in Lock Haven, thirty miles away, remembered her predicament. Twenty years later a newspaper story published details on the occasion of Elaine's Pennsylvania Commonwealth Award:

> *The Lock Haven Express*, April 23, 1963
> **Garth Kleckner, Lock Haven High School band director under whose baton Elaine Shaffer first played the flute as a schoolgirl in this city, remembers an unheralded concert played by the now world-renowned musician, in the most improbable of settings, the American Railway Express office at the Lock Haven station.**
>
> **Elaine Shaffer had just graduated from the Williamsport High School. The time was the early period of World War II. The young musician then had no flute of her own and local arrangements had been put forth to obtain one suitable to her talents.**
>
> **It was finally agreed upon that a silver flute for sale by an agent in Vermont, described as an excellent instrument, and priced at $200, would be sent to Lock Haven for just one hour of tryout by the prospective buyer.**
>
> **As Mr. Kleckner tells it, the instrument came to the American Railway Express office. Elaine and her father, Rex Shaffer, residents of Williamsport, came to try it out. For an hour the young woman, who would later play before world dignitaries, played her concert to the small audience at the station. She was satisfied with the quality of the instrument. Her father made the purchase. A noted musician had bought her first silver flute.**

What of a music school? Without financial help from home a scholarship was crucial. Williamsport's school music director, Osborne Housel, suggested Elaine apply to Eastman School of Music, Peabody, The Julliard School or Indiana University School of Music. None materialized and Mother sat late at night composing futile letters of appeal to local and state politicians. One, addressed to Governor Stevenson, asked for $81 for her daughter to attend a summer program. She believed Elaine's God-given talent would somehow prevail.

A divine plan was unfolding while Elaine pursued her dream. Graduation and her eighteenth birthday passed and, without a teacher, she continued to develop a repertoire of demanding flute music. She listened to classical recordings, especially those of the Philadelphia Orchestra. They were readily available because she made certain to stock them at Housel's Music Store, where she was manager.

In the darkness of our bedroom, Elaine shared her epiphany: "Bev, I know what I want to do. I will make enough money to take the train to Philadelphia and study with that *great man*. Each week it will cost $15 for the train and $15 for the lesson—if he will have me!"

The Curtis Institute of Music and William Kincaid

Elaine composed a lengthy letter to "that great man in Philadelphia," known to her in central Pennsylvania from the weekly radio broadcasts of The Philadelphia Orchestra. Could she imagine the impact it would have on her life?

1138 Vine Ave.
Williamsport, Pa.
December 10, 1943

Mr. William Kincaid
Philadelphia Symphony Orchestra
Philadelphia, Penna.

My dear Mr. Kincaid:
Having heard very much about you, and also having heard you play on the radio and on recordings, I would like to ask you a few questions. In the first place, do you still do private teachings? If so, do you continue this year round? Also, is it necessary to secure an audition in order to study the flute with you?

I am eighteen years old, and a graduate of Williamsport High School, class of 1943, and have been playing the flute for eight years. In this time, it has been my misfortune not to have much private teaching. In other words, I have been helping myself as much as possible, but still feel the need of a good teacher because I know that no one can progress without one. I have a sterling silver flute (Haynes) at the present which is a fine instrument and I like it a lot.

To give you some idea of what I am studying without a teacher: "Sonata" by Pijper; Mozart's 1st and 2nd Concertos; Sonata No. 1 by Bach; 30 Capriccios, by Karg-Elert, and others. I have had considerable experience in bands and orchestras, woodwind ensembles, and solo work on both flute and piccolo. At present I am also studying the piano with a pupil of Ernest Hutcheson.

I would be happy to supply references. If you would like an interview I shall be glad to comply. I certainly would appreciate it if you would consider my request and let me know the details as soon as possible. I am working as manager of the record department of a store in this city, but am very seriously considering resigning from this position if it is possible to have the privilege of studying with you. My ambition is to become a concert artist.

Hoping to hear from you concerning this matter in the near future, I remain,

Very truly yours,
(Miss) H. Elaine Shaffer

The mail promptly brought a brief reply in a small envelope, postmarked Philadelphia.

247 Juniper St.
Philadelphia, Pa.
December 21, 1943

Dear Miss Shaffer:
Please come for an interview and audition on Monday, December 27th at 3.30 at the above address.

Sincerely,
Wm. Kincaid

The apartment door opened and Elaine, along with her father, stood before William Kincaid, a tall gentleman with an imposing, ample white mane that set off a ruddy complexion. His warm handshake and cordial greetings made conversation easy. Elaine took her carefully polished silver instrument from its case, eager to demonstrate the well-rehearsed selections.

How, Kincaid wondered, could Elaine play these difficult numbers, having never had a flute teacher? That question was enough reason for him to accept her as his student. Yes, the invitation to study with William Kincaid sent Elaine home, glowing with anticipation of her next trip to the big city.

At the close of the second lesson, Kincaid asked, "Would you have any interest in a scholarship to the Curtis Institute of Music?" In that moment a world of musical opportunity opened.

Curtis Institute ranked above any music schools she knew—so elite that her high school music director neglected to include it among those he recommended. His upstate Pennsylvania perception was that Curtis was a school for prodigies, geniuses or, the word he used, "weirdos."

The Curtis Institute of Music was founded in 1924, the year before Elaine's birth. Mary Louise Curtis Bok generously endowed it as a conservatory "to train exceptionally gifted young musicians for careers as performing artists on the highest professional level." First chair players of the Philadelphia Orchestra taught its classes and gave private instrumental lessons. Its extensive musical education offered a wide curriculum of demanding subjects, such as Solfege, Counterpoint, Harmony, Conducting, Woodwind Ensemble, etc. Piano study and a language were required.

A full scholarship meant Elaine's sole financial responsibility was room and board. She arrived in January when the first semester was already in operation. Accommodations in Center City Philadelphia were scarce and often lacked space and privacy. Elaine moved from one address to another in the neighborhood of 20th and Pine Streets making sure an angry tenant would not complain of her practice routine.

Jan. 9, 1946

Dear Mother and all,

I was in school all day and didn't have a chance to practice til 6 o'clock. I hardly got started and that man next door turned his radio full blast. I was so mad I got the piccolo and stood by his door and blew it hard and high for about half an hour. It wrecks my lip. I know now to begin at 9.00 am when he leaves and then get 5 hours in by 3.00 pm.

The move to 273 S. 23rd Street suited her need for solitude.

> *Was up to look at the room on 23rd St. Really is super*
> *and only $5.25 a week. It is twice as large as my present*
> *room, has 5 windows with nice lace curtains. Oh, and daily*
> *maid service, clean linens 2 times a week and blankets, etc.*
> *furnished, with sheets. The part I like best is living alone. Two*
> *singers and an oboe player have rooms there.*

Rigorous work in one class following another confirmed Elaine's innate musicality. And yet this newly-come flute student was somewhat of a novelty. Laila Storch, an oboe student, remembers the curious Curtis scene when Elaine arrived. "She made somewhat of a sensation, as she came from 'out in the hills' and yet was totally able to count correctly and follow Tabuteau's difficult instruction."

Marcel Tabuteau, principal oboe of the Philadelphia Orchestra had a demanding European style of pedagogy that was unsettling. Elaine first met him as conductor of the woodwind class.

Jan. 27, 1945

> *Dear Bev,*
>
>   *I wish you could meet this Mr. Tabuteau. He is sort of*
> *the tough-but-oh-so-gentle type. One minute he is yelling*
> *and swearing in French and the next minute he cracks a*
> *joke and then everyone laughs. Everyone really likes him. We*
> *got started and he began yelling at another flute player. He*
> *said, "Let theez leetle girl play." I was shaking in my shoes.*
> *So I started—he stopped in a few minutes and looked at me.*
> *"That was very goot flute. Where did you come from? You*
> *have practiced this music before, no?" I said, "No sir, I've*
> *never seen it before." Then after that he stopped again and*
> *said, "With whom did you study before you came here?" I*
> *said, "I didn't have a teacher, except a clarinet teacher." Then*
> *one of the clarinet players said, "Maybe we should take lessons*
> *from a flute player."*

Elaine soon learned that a compliment in that class was a rarity.

Stellar faculty musicians such as William Kincaid and Marcel Tabuteau were accessible to students, but it was the rich camaraderie of collegial friendships that supported one another on the path to professional careers. Classmates like Laila Storch, a student of Tabuteau, and Marilyn Costello, studying harp with Edna Phillips, encouraged Elaine to circulate in places where musicians gathered and to "get to know the right people." The Latimer Deli back of the Academy was a likely spot.

The years at Curtis were highlighted by the weekly private lessons with Kincaid. He encouraged her with his personal commendations and inspired her pursuit of a concert career. Scheduled lessons had priority over her academic and social life. Each week, she framed her hours around personal practice in preparation for meeting her teacher. Furthermore, she required adequate rest and nourishment. Her mind must be clear and relaxed to play her best.

Elaine disciplined her social life as much as her music training and considered parties frivolous and dating a waste of time, especially if she detected a fellow's disinterest in music. She accepted ginger ale, while others drank beer. This practice elicited the comment, "a rare student who doesn't emulate her teacher's use of alcohol."

First and second chair orchestral positions were choice opportunities for valuable experience. Kincaid recommended her as a summer placement in the Robin Hood Dell Orchestra, where she was the youngest member—and only woman, except for the harpist. The Dell ensemble, made up largely of Philadelphia Orchestra members, was conducted by Dimitri Mitropoulis in the summer of 1945.

The Reyburn Plaza concerts were another well-attended summer series held in Philadelphia's Center City. Elaine played second chair and welcomed the fee to augment what she got from teaching a few private students.

Just as opportunities to make music increased, questions and confusion about the sacrifices and narrow focus of a lifelong career in music plagued Elaine. Her journals and letters poured out her struggles to make sense of life, her years at Curtis, and her future direction. Social, psychological and spiritual turmoil denied her a schoolgirl's exuberance. Self-doubt, dissatisfaction, and the ever-present concern for "time slipping by" dominated her spirit, especially with graduation looming and no full employment on the horizon. Conflicting demands on her time and energy made clear that she preferred nothing more than hours of playing her instrument, if only she did not have to interject time to earn a living as a clerk at Wanamaker's Department Store or Shryock's Music Store.

"One day I am selling moth balls and coat hangars and the next day I am a musician."

A popular neighborhood church gave her a measure of security. She joined students from various colleges and universities who gathered for the urban hospitality, stimulating programs and sermons of a popular teacher/ preacher. Rational, intelligent messages were persuasive calls to seek God's will. "Full time Christian service," heralded week after week, would mean a life as a missionary, probably in a foreign country.

None of this was lost on Elaine and, in fact, was reminiscent of impressionable earlier years in her hometown Baptist church. She had no doubt that her unique musical talent was God-given, and wanted to use it to honor her deep faith.

Elaine's beauty and devout lifestyle attracted several young men of the church group. She enjoyed their company, their shared values, and especially the attention of one handsome seminarian. Was this her "rescuing prince"? If his goal was to "save the world," Elaine was ideally suited to be his partner.

Romantic expectations sustained and then distracted her until the fervor of the relationship waned as each of the young couple identified their individual passion. Elaine emerged from her confusion with a realization of her real calling and greatest satisfaction, to perform music from her heart.

Welcome relief from persistent introspection came with the rite of passage at Curtis. Mr. Kincaid encouraged the traditional graduation recital to showcase her accomplishments.

She chose the Mozart *Concerto* to perform before her peers, the faculty and her family.

> *Dear Folks,*
> *My recital is May 2 at 5.15 (not AM). There is a violinist and pianist on the program, too. The violinist is Norman Carol—you saw him in the W. Wind recital last year. He played the Bach double with that girl. He is very good looking. I am playing the Mozart Concerto and am first on the program to get it over.*

The final days at Curtis found her conflicted in several areas.

<u>**May 2, 1947**</u> I spent the morning at a lesson with Kincaid—he is so wonderful. Had an ill feeling all afternoon, not expecting to sound like much at the recital. The Mozart went magnificently—all this I feel is

Divine power to allow me to do such a perfect performance. It amazed me in some places—it was the best I have ever played anywhere.

May 5 Practiced and feel quite pleased with my progress. Everything I play sounds better and more confident since the recital. Doug Kent said it was the most musical performance that ever happened in Curtis. Am still hearing about how pleased Mr. Kincaid was. How I love him and wish to please him.

May 9 Can't believe that officially this was my last day of Curtis. Get tears in my eyes every time I think of leaving Mr. Kincaid and Mr. Tabuteau. Outside of those, the school means very little to me. The orchestra concert was beautiful. Having parents to witness makes it that much more enjoyable. Mr. Serkin was wonderful in the "Emperor" Concerto.

May 10 This was the "big day" at Curtis. Such a feeling of mixed emotions. I wasn't affected much, except when Mrs. Zimbalist talked about the faculty. Have thought of Mr. Kincaid constantly since the recital and miss him terribly.

The Kincaids soon left for their Maine summer retreat. Students emptied the practice rooms and left classrooms for home, but Elaine remained to spend her summer in an unrelenting search for full-time employment as a musician.

Summer of Despond

*"It's not easy sitting on uncertainty,
but I am beginning to make friends with it."*

"ONLY MEN WANTED" stated The Baltimore Symphony in its call for auditions. That bias shared world-round at the time Elaine tried to be heard changed. Today auditioning musicians play behind a curtain and so there is anonymity. But in 1947 the symphony was a boy's club.

Elaine appeared before many: the Philadelphia Youth Concert, the National Symphony, the Cleveland Symphony, the North Carolina Symphony, and the Denver Symphony. None elicited hope. Kincaid sent her name to the Los Angeles Symphony for a first flute opening, to no avail.

A first flute position in the Pittsburgh Symphony under Fritz Reiner was an opening that excited her. In a letter home: *This is the one I really want—it's first flute, a wonderful opportunity, good conductor and I've written two letters. I know Reiner hates girls but maybe Billy* [Kincaid] *or Ormandy could do something.*

This springtime of "uncertainty" seemed relentless in her journal.

May 15 Went to the Academy of Music this morning for a Youth Concert audition. Haven't practiced much lately. Played very well under the circumstances. Only board member I recognized was Edna Phillips. They talked while I was playing—not very courteous.

May 16 Called N.Y. and will have Pittsburgh audition on May 26. Have found new hope about a job . . .

May 17 Advised a young female student to go to college instead of trying to become a musician. Right now I feel almost constrained to give the same advice to any aspiring musician.

16

May 19 This was my last lesson, but I didn't cry. I couldn't even get near Mr. Kincaid to kiss him on the cheek. Well, Cleveland is out—only thing left is Pittsburgh. And maybe this summer at the Dell playing the Gesensway. (I think my goose is cooked. Mitropoulos wants his *man*.)

May 22 Feel more sure of sight-reading and this afternoon it occurred to me that I can go after this job with confidence, whatever comes of it. Miss my teacher so much. (My pupil, Searl Freedman, was accepted by William as a next year student!)

May 24 The heat has overtaken the temperaments of Philadelphians. I walk to Rittenhouse Square to enjoy the restful atmosphere. But today I practiced all day. I must not under rate [sic] my ability any more than to over rate [sic] it. I have been thinking too lightly of my ability.

In a letter home, Elaine wrote: *The audition for Washington offered me a job—2nd flute. It's a job, but I'd like to get something better than Washington.*

May 26 Felt quite confident about my playing in N.Y. but first the setback. When I arrived they told me that Reiner wouldn't listen to me for first (chair). Then waited for almost three hours and had to talk with him for awhile before he would even let me play. After that I was so beaten that I just wanted to go somewhere and cry my eyes out. It was humiliation and made me wonder what kind of a democracy this is. Felt so alone in my disappointment.

Elaine wrote very little about this audition for flute with The Pittsburgh Symphony and the outcome of this crushing personal ordeal. The reality of her gender was, of course, insurmountable. Musical artistry to her seemed to be lost on those in high positions. She later learned that the position of third flute was also open, yet Reiner concluded, after these hours, "You are the best I have heard, but too bad you are a woman."

Another trailblazer, unknown to Elaine, Frances Blaisdell, 1912-2009, faced rejections while seeking positions in musical organizations in New York City. "In 1937 she was refused an audition for an opening in the New York Philharmonic because she was a woman." Douglas Martin, *New York Times*, March 31, 2009

May 27 Unpleasant morning spent playing exercises and crying in between measures (and then) Mrs. Kincaid called and offered to give me their apartment for the summer and I accepted after some thought.

That summer of 1947, during college, I shared that apartment with Elaine and found summer employment in Philadelphia. On our day off, mine as a waitress, and hers from John Wanamaker's, we took bus trips to the seashore, enjoyed concerts at the Robin Hood Dell, played tennis, attended her church, and talked for hours. My presence, I believe, relieved her loneliness as we untangled our plans and prospects for the future. On many evenings Elaine sat mending Kincaid's vast collection of music. This was, to her, a practical gesture toward giving something of value to her beloved teacher. We sat in the very room of his home, she reminded me, where he opened to her the doors of the Curtis Institute of Music.

Nostalgia for summers gone by lingered during Philadelphia's heat and humidity. In 1944 there had been idyllic days in Maine when Elaine studied with Mr. Kincaid several days a week. She also had time for long swims in Little Lake Sebago, lake cruises in the Chris Craft, and leisurely shoreline fishing.

Another summer, she represented Curtis' woodwind section at the Berkshire Music Festival, under conductor Sergei Koussevitsky. The eight-week summer season in The Robin Hood Dell Orchestra under Dimitri Mitropoulis was a valuable opportunity to learn flute parts and solos in important symphonic works.

These final Philadelphia summer evenings found her in the audience at the Dell after the day's stifling heat of John Wanamaker's Department Store. Music making, reduced to playing the Reyburn Plaza concerts, was a humbling concession since she was second chair to one of her students, Eleanor Mitchell.

July 17 The things I most desire have become 100 times more precious to me. Now I realize that I would rather be doing the most menial thing in music than to spend 8 hours in a store being ruled by someone. That bodily fatigue is stunting my breath control. It is so frustrating to know that being an artist that no one will listen to and getting started is so hard. I must be willing to be unrecognized.

August 8 Played well at the Plaza, but felt subdued to play with E. M. as first. It would be good but for her intonation. Felt rather rebellious but then I remember that I am fortunate to be playing at all and count it a blessing.

August 20 Have decided that having a routine job is really good for me. It makes me realize the value of time and I accomplish more now than before. It is true that activity is conducive to contentment.

Affirmation mingled with the gloom of summer. Elaine received word of her appointment as Alternate Flute with the Philadelphia Orchestra. Her name would be listed on their fall season's program. The alternate attended the orchestra's rehearsals and filled in for an ill or absent flutist.

August 27 Still have the question in my mind about my future, whether it is better to keep on as I have or to make a complete break. This is the time to do it if any time.

September 1 Flute playing sounds better than it has for all of the summer. This is the day that Mr. Kincaid begins to work. I should like to see him—it will not be long now. I anticipate studying this winter and really improving as an artist.

A rambling letter addressed "to maitre" followed this final journal entry after the bland summer. Mother, once more, heard Elaine's litany of self doubt—if she had been born other than a female—a failure and disappointment to her family—not worthy of the "sacrifice" they had made. These sentiments weakened Elaine's resolve and elicited Mother's "tough love" response.

In the midst of Mother's daily housekeeping chores and her care for the family at home, letters from Elaine seemed to have lost their focus. Mother allowed no sympathy for the oppressive summer heat, the dimming of Elaine's vision, or the absence of promising offers. She wrote:

> *Dear Elaine,*
>
> *If you can't realize God put you in this world as a girl because that's what he wanted you to be and gave you musical talent because he wanted you to have it, you had better throw the flute, music and everything away. The fact that you have had a chance to study music and graduate from Curtis was what I wanted for you.*

Do you stop to think how grateful we can be for all the Lord's blessings as long as they are coming in the form we want? When they stop flowing we forget the ones we had.

Any sacrifice we made is nothing because they are blessings from the Lord. As for calling yourself a failure, that is ridiculous. It makes me think of the narrow escapes you have had all your life—and I could name them. I am convinced you have let the business of being a girl grow to be more than it is. Many men musicians do not have jobs, you have told me, and I imagine some of them are good and have been trying longer than you. And they don't have someone like K. or O. to write recommendations.

Am hoping you will look at all this from a higher view.

Lots of love,
Mother

A month later in central Pennsylvania, October's bright blue weather illuminated the glorious fall foliage. The world had changed. Mother's letters are now addressed to 3424 Baltimore St., Kansas City, MO., with maternal instructions to find a good doctor to give her a "nerve tonic," not a "sleeping pill," and to eat nutritious food when she is eating out.

Elaine began the fall season of 1947 as second flute in the Kansas City Philharmonic, under conductor Efrem Kurtz. A transformation of her life began!

Symphony Life: Kansas City Philharmonic

Efrem Kurtz, conductor of the Kansas City Philharmonic, had an opening as he faced his fall concert season. His quest for second flute led to Philadelphia, the Curtis Institute, William Kincaid and to Elaine. Kurtz first learned of Elaine from young members of his orchestra who had been colleagues at Curtis. They spoke of her outstanding reputation in Philadelphia, her artistry and accomplishments, memorable from student days. Elaine's close friend, oboist Laila Storch, was enthusiastically supported by Curtis' Nathan Brusilow, Gaetano Molieri, Clem Barone, David Colvig, and Marion Davies.

Initial contacts for the position made no mention of an audition. A collegial entrée into the symphonic world was assured once Kurtz made a phone call to Elaine's teacher. Lavish with expressions of confidence in Elaine's remarkable capabilities as a professional musician, William Kincaid said, "Elaine is certainly the most talented student I have ever taught."

Elaine's trip to Kansas City, Missouri, her very first by air, excited her as a new and exciting way of transportation in 1948. The westward flight carried her beyond the mountains and forests of Pennsylvania that she had taken for granted. Kansas City was far from her hometown of Williamsport, her Altoona birthplace, Philadelphia's Rittenhouse Square, Logan Circle, the Curtis Institute and the Academy of Music. She worried that the distance might change her relationship established with Kincaid, whose teachings and affirmations continued to be the fixed star in her galaxy.

At first Elaine's misgivings delayed her response to Kurtz and the Kansas City Philharmonic. She decided to drive a bold and risky bargain. Before signing a contract, she asked not only for more money, but for time to fulfill a previous engagement. More boldly, she asked for the promise of a concerto solo appearance within the orchestra's first season. Claude Monteux was secure in the position of first flute. First flutes usually play the solos. Elaine was assigned to second chair. How would Monteux feel about Elaine's solo?

Kurtz conceded on all points and Elaine arrived in Kansas City in time for the rehearsals and October opening of the twenty-week season. Philadelphia promoters and friends welcomed her as well as the fellow musicians; she felt at ease with this unfamiliar conductor.

Maestro Kurtz was a tall, slim, elegant Continental who looked the part of an imposing impresario. Not yet fifty years old, his graying hair hung loosely over his ears. His daily rehearsal uniform was a navy blue blazer over a dark cashmere sweater or cotton turtle-neck shirt. A long black or seasonal camel-hair overcoat with dangling sleeves hung over his shoulders, a distinctive European statement in this midwestern city. Russian born, he had been conducting the Kansas City Philharmonic since 1943. His peripatetic energy endeared Kurtz to his young players, average age of twenty-eight. Once his wife made clear her preference for life in New York City, he hosted enjoyable evenings in his apartment in the company of musicians and guest artists.

The Kurtz gatherings introduced Elaine to a whirl of socializing, unknown in her disciplined routine and loneliness as a student in Philadelphia. Orchestra peers, including the eleven Curtis colleagues, welcomed the chance to relax following evening concerts, especially with visiting guest soloists.

As the maestro became acquainted with his orchestra's newest additions, he asked the Curtis crowd what they knew of Elaine. "She's a wholesome type of person" was the general consensus. Kurtz, with his Russian background, easily misinterpreted the English phrase. He amused them when he differed, "She is not homely at all!"

Adjusting to this new and expansive world did not diminish Elaine's fond remembrance of beloved connections with Philadelphia. Those early weeks found her tearful as she read and re-read letters from her dear friend and former roommate, Marilyn Costello, now first harp with the Philadelphia Orchestra. Marilyn's inimitable humor bonded their friendship and became a timely gift that sparked news and gossip from that former life, especially at the Academy of Music where paths crossed with William Kincaid.

Worcester, Mass.
October 17, 1947

Dearest Elaine,

I was so glad to get your letter. Billy has been saying, "Heard from Elaine yet?" for several days, besides making signs of weeping back and forth each time I see him. Yesterday, I triumphantly started to tell him that I got a letter. He said he did, too, and we were both happy.

Naturally we are so sad that you're not with us (Billy and I have the same sentiments regarding you). But it really is better for you, even though I know how you feel. Cheer up, Elaine. You are such a wonderful girl, such a good, deserving girl, all things will work out for the best for you. Everyone you've ever met has had no trouble at all in finding out immediately that you are an unusually capable and outstanding person.

Billy said that he has already written a letter to Kurtz telling him that you play "the" Mozart so beautifully you should play it. ("The" Mozart what? "Eine Kleine Nachtmusik" maybe.)

I think of you so much of the time. I was going to use "Dear darling Elaine" for a salutation, but I was afraid someone might see it and start to talk.

The world is noisy enough as it is . . .

All my love to you, sweet girl,
Marilyn

Phila. Pa.
Oct. 26th

Dear Elaine,

You were so sweet to write me those two letters to the Green Room (Dear Green Room). I read one last night during the concert. On the stage, naturally. I'm so glad to hear you're so well liked by your conductor. Boy! He's lucky to have you. Billy and I discuss you every time we see one another. He's so happy when I get a letter.

He says he thinks it's fine for you to be there because if things go well there they'll go well anywhere and you just have to be away. He said that he will write to you soon. He was waiting until you were more settled and stopped crying. Don't worry, I'm keeping the flame burning for you, although it would burn without me, it's so well kindled.

Kurtz really must be mad about you. It's so nice to hear of your pleasant times there. Don't be concerned about a lack of nice men. Let's not worry until we're older! Next year.

We miss you dear. I don't do anything but practice and eat, sometimes both at the same time. Also sleep, while I practice. Say hello to Laila for me.

Love,
Marilyn

A break in the Kansas City schedule allowed Elaine to fly to Chicago for a brief but comforting reunion with Marilyn Costello and William Kincaid and the touring Philadelphia Orchestra.

Dear Mother and Dad,

It is midnight but I want to write a quick note to tell you the Chicago trip was a great success. Flying is really thrilling.

Spent all day Saturday with Billy and have never had such a wonderful time in my life. He was so unrestrained and friendly that it was easy to talk with him. We talked all day and the time really flew, as it has a habit of doing when you don't want it to. He is very happy about the good news here and believes it was good to come. Before Saturday I had always admired him as a colleague and friend, so different from the student-teacher relationship. He said at the rate I am going he is thinking of taking lessons with me.

We had two rehearsals today and I am just dead—was over at Kurtz's tonight listening to records and eating. He is listening to me play the Mozart on Thursday—we are playing on Orchestras of the Nation in December and January. I suggested he play the Mozart Flute Concerto and he said that is a good idea. What a break if he does it because the program is nation-wide NBC.

We have another subscription concert tomorrow night— Nathan Milstein is playing. The first flute player is really worried here—he is getting to be a neurotic. I always play

*the solos backstage so he hears and gets more nervous—it's a
mean trick, but Billy said he used to do it!*

*Love,
Elaine*

A mutually memorable day in Chicago pleased the Philadelphia
visitors.

After Chicago

Dearest Dear of all dears,

*Elaine it was so wonderful to see you. You are such an
unusual person, like a rare breath of air. On Sunday we had
some of "the boys" in our room on the train (we tripped them
in the corridors and they fell in). We were discussing you.
Billy and I just sat and talked about how wonderful you are,
with and without the flute. Ward said that he just loves to
stand and watch you smile. But then, I musn't tell you these
things, or your hood will not fit.(ha, ha, joke)*

Tell Laila I send my friendly regard. Be Good.

M.C.

William Kincaid's tone and signature became lighthearted.

Dear Elaine,

*Many thanks for your letters and I am glad to know that
you enjoy the concerts over the air.*

*E. K. called and we had a pleasant talk and of course he
raved about you.*

*I am busy as ever and have managed to keep almost up
with my Curtis teaching, only five hours behind at present.*

*It seems a long time since Chicago but the memory of
that day is very clear.*

*Good bye for now,
Bill*

Hotel Statler, D.C.

*A great big hello to my star student and thanks for the
weather report and the telegram. The concert went well and*

on Saturday night I was almost satisfied. The enclosed notices may interest you.

No pleasant weather has been experienced since that beautiful day in Chicago and the forecast is not reassuring.

As ever,
Bill

Extensive travel by members of the Philadelphia Orchestra never interfered with the faithful correspondence from Marilyn Costello and Bill Kincaid.

Phila., Pa.

Dear Elaine,
I had a little talk with "Blue Eyes" Kincaid the other night on the way home from New York. He says that you're neglecting him. He's afraid your "regards" is fading. I assured him it isn't. He talked about you. Before I tell you, go out and buy a larger babushka. He said you are the best pupil he's ever had. We discussed your progress and industry and talent. He says some people let talent prove detrimental, but you took advantage of yours and really listened, worked and applied everything he taught you. Our only conclusion was that you're pretty good.

He also discussed your pleasant manner etc. He likes you so much! He asked me about your love life. At that point the train went under a tunnel and all went blank. I'm kidding. He says you're so "imaginative." What's that got to do with boyfriends? I know, you, (meaning I) can imagine you (meaning I) have a boyfriend.

If I don't stop this foolishness, I'll find the Orchestra in Charleston, W. Va., or rather I'll find myself here, with them there. "Them there" = good grammar.

Bye, dear love,
Mccccc

247 South Juniper St.
Philadelphia, PA
January 1, 1948

Dear Elaine,

This is the first letter of the year to anyone and we all wish you a Happy New Year and hope that your Christmas was a happy one.

The package which you so thoughtfully sent arrived in fine shape and we enjoyed the candy, nuts, and fruit cake with great gusto. Many thanks.

We are busy as usual but manage to keep in good health although a few weeks ago I completely lost my voice and was unable to torture my poor pupils with my vocal attempts. In fact I had to stand for an over abundance of the most unusual flute sounds ever invented, without a dissenting vote.

We think of the lovely Elaine all the time and send our love and best wishes to her.

Sincerely,
Bill

The concerto solo, included in Elaine's negotiations with Maestro Kurtz, was scheduled for January 21, 1948. Mother's visit to Kansas City and her presence in the audience was not enough to allay Elaine's "extreme nervous apprehension."

January 22, 1948

Dear Daddie,

Enclosed is the notice of last night's concert. Many thanks for your morale-building note. That, with a couple of telegrams from Marilyn and Goradetskys, and a long distance phone call from The Bill's (Kincaid), all helped to remedy my extreme nervous apprehension a few hours before.

Generally, I was quite happy about the performance—feeling very comfortable on the stage and good support from Kurtz and the orchestra. The audience was spontaneous and (for Kansas City) almost enthusiastic.

There is the usual let-down feeling of the "day after," so I have taken it easy . . .

Orchestra tours throughout the state brought live concert experiences to communities far from Kansas City. Train travel allowed for important business conversation.

February 5, 1948

Dear Mother and all,

We arrived in K.C. at 8.10 this morning, and I feel too tired to work. We had a good trip—Kansas towns all look alike. Next week we go to St. Joseph—that's not so far. It was pretty exciting yesterday, as Kurtz and Henderson (manager) carried on their business on the train, deciding who is coming back next season, and who is fired, etc. Anyhow, it is definite now about Laila and me and he had no trouble at all . . . H. was very happy that (Kurtz) wanted me for first flute. Also, Monteux would have been out anyway as the union asked to have him fired, for what reason I don't know.

There was a good crowd last nite [sic] at the concert. I almost fell asleep having only slept a half hour in the afternoon. They had a bright spotlight on the stage and it gave everyone headaches—we couldn't see very well. Laila said there were spots in front of her eyes. Tustin said, "They're not spots—they're the notes."

Love,
Elaine

As the Kansas City Philharmonic finished the concert season of 1947-48, Laila Storch, principal oboe, remembered, "We barely earned enough to survive." Secure summer employment took Elaine to California to join the Hollywood Bowl Symphony under Eugene Ormandy, its guest conductor. A new world in California contrasted with much of Elaine's earlier life experience. This unique opening expanded Elaine's horizon and spoke of William Kincaid's genuine interest in advancing her career.

Symphony Life: Hollywood Bowl Symphony

"You're not in Kansas anymore." F. Baum <u>Wizard of Oz</u>

The Hollywood Bowl Symphony had engaged Eugene Ormandy to conduct its 1948 summer season. He wanted William Kincaid, his first flute in Philadelphia, to take that place in California. However, Kincaid found the prospects of eight weeks in Hollywood no match for a summer at his idyllic cottage in Maine. Instead he promoted Elaine as fully qualified for this assignment. Perhaps Maestro Ormandy recalled the day in Philadelphia when Kincaid sang Elaine's praises. "You must do something for her, Gene." His response: "But, she's a woman!" Now the conductor took those solid words to heart.

This dazzling opening had advantages beyond summer employment for Elaine: the experience of living in California, learning more of the first flute repertoire, and playing under Ormandy. The short Kansas City season allowed her to begin the California residency requirement for membership in the musicians union in Los Angeles. Kincaid understood an impractical but important protocol such as key contacts that Elaine learned after her arrival in California.

> *February 24, 1948*
>
> *Dear Elaine,*
>
> *So your season is drawing to a close and you will be moving further west soon. Too bad you can't pay Philadelphia a visit beforehand.*
>
> *When you arrive in L.A. write a note to Mr. Philip Kahgan c/o Paramount Studios and tell him I wish to be remembered to him and that you are the one I spoke to him*

about. You must be circumspect as you well know. Mr. E. O. knows and hasn't forgotten. Also please send your new address.

I will be seeing you about May 18 but you will hear from me before then.

With all good wishes for the best of luck and know that I am always thinking about you.

Sincerely,
Bill

March 16, 1948

Dear Elaine,

Enclosed you will find the programs you requested. Of course do not show the list to anyone.

It has been suggested you keep pretty much to yourself and steer clear of Doriot Anthony, a former student of mine who is interested in the summer season.

Excuse the short note but I must catch the train to N.Y. Best wishes as always,

Sincerely,
Bill

Elaine attended concerts of the Los Angeles Philharmonic but avoided meeting musicians who may have questioned her presence in L.A. just when summer assignments were being made. Letters outside were limited, even though her silence might have been misunderstood.

3268 Bennett Blvd.
Hollywood 28 Calif.

Dear Mother and Dad,

Friday afternoon I went to the L.A. Philharmonic and saw Wallenstein conduct for the first time—I certainly would not like to play with him. He conducts like a finely regulated metronome. No warmth or expression. I avoided meeting any of the musicians but did speak to Torello—he used to play bass in the Phila. Orch. and I had forgotten that he was here. After the concert I saw Albert Tipton on the street (he didn't see me). If you remember he used to play 2nd flute in

> *Phila. and is now 1ˢᵗ in St. Louis. You can imagine what I thought of immediately when I saw him—as he is very good and has had more experience than I. At first I was a little upset as I thought of being double crossed before—and he is the one who took my job at the Dell in 1946. But after thinking it over I decided it is impossible as I have a verbal promise from the manager and according to the union it is as good as a contract. Maybe Tipton is working on something for next year.*

In the meantime, news from Kansas City—Kurtz' resignation and plans for the next season in Houston—were passed along to Mother. Elaine will occupy first chair in Houston.

> *It looks like we will go to Houston after all. They have conceded to the ultimatum—now the only trouble is to get out of the K.C. contract—Kurtz thinks there will not be any difficulty. Laila is going to France—Marion went to Boston to audition for Koussevitsky for first chair cello. He had a designer in Paris design dresses for the Houston girls and is going to send it and I should have it made in L.A. He sent all the programs of Houston—I've got enough to worry about now without <u>them</u>.*
>
> *Heard from E.K. and he is just raving about Kincaid's playing in the orchestra in N.Y. He never heard anything like it. He (E) had been telling me my tone would have to be bigger to play first flute practically all last season—so much that I have a complex about it. So he discusses the matter with Kincaid and I guess Kincaid put him straight on it. He said if you try to force a tone into a bigger one it kills it—then said my tone is big and the quality will develop with maturity and experience playing first. Kurtz was just judging from that one day that I played first—and I didn't even have any solos to play.*

The California climate and lifestyle were conducive to a leisurely springtime. Elaine continued to practice, prepared the summer music, took art classes, and enjoyed occasional duo musical sessions. She took advantage of the pool and sun at the home of John and Dolly Stofer, located in the Hollywood Hills. They welcomed Elaine to the neighborhood and toured her in and around Los Angeles.

A Scottish Skye Terrier, seemingly unattached, now became an affectionate companion to Elaine: *He comes and puts his head on the pillow. Then too when I am practicing he lies right beside the music stand. He has black hair but after I give him a bath I shall probably find out why his name is "Brownie."*

Efrem Kurtz arrived in Los Angeles on assignment as conductor to participate in the making of the movie "Macbeth" with Orson Welles. The visit was a diversion for Elaine. Kurtz brought news about plans for next season in Houston. Elaine assisted in auditioning 12 violinists for Houston. It gave her perspective on the conductor's hiring procedure.

Another orchestra on Elaine's mind, "The" Philadelphia Orchestra, headed to California on their west coast tour. Very soon she would have a reunion with dear friends. A special train with twelve cars and three engines toured them across country to San Diego. For Elaine, weeks of a relaxed California schedule, regular exercise, and abundant sunshine reap compliments from Philadelphians.

> *Dear Mother,*
>
> *It was a big thrill to hear the orchestra and see everyone. Hardly anyone recognized me at first and they all say I have changed. Hilsberg's eyes were popping and said to Kincaid, "Beely, she is beautiful!"*
>
> *There is no need to say how happy I was to see Bill and I must say the feeling was mutual. I can tell you more of these eventful days when I see you. Anyway we talked about many things—when I left him at the station, he seemed a little shaken and said he is changed and implied that he would not drink so much. I told him I prayed for him and he said, "Don't stop now, I really need it." So many times he told me never to drink—he said, "It will ruin you. I know." I played for him and feel much better about that—I was definitely in a rut and slightly off the track. He said he expected this—as it usually happens right after you leave your teacher—but then you finally find yourself and it is original then.*
>
> *Kincaid is going to sell me his Powell silver flute soon as Powell sends his new one. Also he said he is going to will*

me his platinum one! I played his platinum one and it really knocks me out. What an instrument!

Marilyn looks fine but she has had a lot of tough luck lately. She fell off a bicycle that broke in two while in Ann Arbor—her face was cut, but she looks OK now. Ormandy said he would fire her if she ever did that again.

Am inspired to work now and feel like a different person since seeing Bill—have to play for E.O. in two weeks—he knew I was at the concerts but did not speak to him.

Write soon.

Elaine

This appointment continued to involve cautious public and private strategy behind the scenes

Dear Mother,

Everything is still up in the air here. In the meantime, I am working 7 hours a day and getting more nervous by the minute.

Dr. Wecker (manager of the Bowl) called me last week and said in a very formal voice, "The union has informed me that you are a flutist of wide experience—Mr. Ormandy will be here to hold auditions next week. Are you interested?" I have spoken with him several times since I am here and he explained the situation thoroughly—and suddenly he is so very formal as if he never knew me. I saw both him and Ormandy while the orchestra was here and both of them completely ignored me—because there were men standing around. The thing Dr. W. has done is to wait until my three months were up and then called the union and said, "Look here, it's late and you will not allow us to import a flute player. How about giving me a list of eligible people who have just transferred into the local—in that way the union gave him my name and everything is perfectly legal. So now I am waiting for E.O. to get here. This is a war of nerves. I will wire you the moment everything is clear. In the meantime, DON'T say anything.

The hide-and-seek game ended with the audition. Elaine sent the promised wire to her family with details to follow.

> *Dear Mother and Dad and all,*
>
> *I am still shaking. Please excuse the writing. The audition was this afternoon at 3 PM at the Bowl executive offices. There were several other musicians there when I arrived including the 1st bassoon of K.C. I was called in first and E.O. was very nice, and was glad to "meet" me. Also Dr. Wecker was very formal as if we had never met.*
>
> *I had to play quite a lot and all difficult things—also listening were Dr. Wecker and Mr. Pometti—the contractor for the Bowl and the L.A. Philharmonic. Everything went well and I played better than my normal self so everyone was duly impressed. Afterwards I went outside and talked with Mr. Pometti and signed the contract on the spot—the publicity manager came and asked questions about hometown and training, etc. Oh, while playing I looked at Ormandy all the time (he was beating) as I knew the music from memory. He said, "Do you always look at the conductor like that when you play? We should get along very well—conductors like to be watched."*
>
> *I wore my new white suit—I think that is what knocked them out!*
>
> *I don't care what you say for the newspaper—but think it is wise just to say I was engaged by Eugene Ormandy as first flutist of the Hollywood Bowl Symphony Orchestra—season beginning July 13th with five concerts each week for 8 weeks. Nationwide broadcast every Sunday over CBS. In August I will be featured in Debussy's "Prelude to the Afternoon of a Faun."*
>
> *First rehearsal is July 10th at 9.00 AM. Getting up at 6.30 should not be too hard. They have rehearsals early because it gets so hot here in the afternoon. It was plenty warm today, but they had a fan going where I played.*
>
> *Write to me soon.*
>
> *Love,*
Elaine

The success of the audition, a signed contract in hand, the cherished memory of the springtime reunion with the Philadelphia Orchestra, and Kincaid's mentoring, eased the early days of rehearsal. She gained familiarity with the "feeling of the orchestra, balance, etc." Kincaid's wire, "Your complete success and happiness most important to me," hung on her wall. The mail delivered details of the first day's rehearsal.

> *Dear Mother and all,*
>
> *Today was the big day. I feel like an old worn out wash rag after this morning. I was sitting there saying to myself during the whole rehearsal, "What a way to make a living!" This is without a doubt the hardest job and the biggest nervous strain of my whole life. After this season I will weigh about 20 pounds less and there will probably be an appreciable addition to the white hair! Hope that I will not always be so nervous as today. Of course everyone else was too. Ormandy was very nice and made a big speech saying he had a <u>standard</u>, namely, his <u>other</u> orchestra. I felt like saying, "You're expecting <u>Kincaid</u>, yet?" One work we played was the Phila. Orch parts and Billy's marks were all over; that made me feel more at home—sort of proximity. At about five minutes before the rehearsal started I wished Billy were there to hold my hand—but then decided I was a big girl now.*
>
> *Must close now and write a note to Bill—he was probably as nervous as I today.*

Butterflies, followed by gratifying, even thrilling, experiences, began the opening night of "Symphony under the Stars." The Mendelssohn *Nocturne and Scherzo* were selected in a program **"more poetic than bombastic."** *The Los Angeles Times* front page review, surrounded by photos of members of society attending the event, greeted Elaine the morning of July 14, 1948: **"The *Scherzo* came off with an agreeable show of well-controlled curiosity and Ormandy called upon Elaine Shaffer to acknowledge applause for her brightly played flute solo."**

July 14, 1948

Dear Mother and Dad and all,

Just a note to enclose review of last night's concert. I am very happy, and think I have reason to be so. It's not every day you are on the front page!

The rehearsal went fine and the orchestra stamped their feet and yelled when I finished the Mendelssohn Scherzo. I could not eat last night. I have lost already 4 pounds—down to 133 now. But after arriving at the Bowl there were no nerves left and I was quite calm. All the time I wished you all could be there and Billy and Efrem. You would have been happy to hear how I played and how the orchestra sounded. Ormandy is a real inspiration and all I have to do is watch him and everything goes. The Bowl is a <u>beautiful</u> place—no comparison to the Dell. There was a moon and everything was perfect, even the weather. After the Scherzo the orchestra yelled Bravo and Ormandy was beaming. This was the biggest thrill of my life and what I have waited for. I have sent a review to Bill and told him <u>he</u> was responsible.

All my love and gratitude to you for making everything possible.

Elaine

There are bittersweet moments when letters are grossly inadequate. Elaine's stunning performances before a responsive public were too seldom shared in the company of those closest to her.

Dear Mother and Dad,

Just a note as there is a lot of music to look over. There is so much new music, and most of it I am playing for the 1ˢᵗ time.

Want to tell you what Ormandy said to me today. By the way, this was the 3ʳᵈ rehearsal and I feel more and more in command of the situation and completely devoid of nervousness.

Today the Columbia men were there testing for the broadcast Sunday. There are so many mikes in front of me I'm sure to be heard! At intermission E.O. called me over to podium and the control said the flute was too soft in opening of Ravel's "Bolero"—I said I could give more and E.O. said to him, "You tune it up in the control room. She is playing it exactly as I want it." At the rehearsal he was having everyone phrase the "Bolero" same as I had done. There really is a big advantage in listening to Bill all these years!

Saw Dr. Wecker (mgr. of the Bowl) in the bank today and he said, "I have not had a chance to tell you—you played beautifully—Kincaid was quite right." You can imagine how happy I was to hear that—especially from him. Billy will be glad to hear it too.

Dear Folks,

I do hope you have heard the broadcast today. Last night we played the same things plus some soloists. Ormandy called me before the broadcast and said I had played as never before and that everything he had said was lacking was there. Today he was very happy too, <u>and</u> said the cadenza in "Tales from Vienna Woods" I played just the way he wanted it (strictly my own interpretation, too) and said that Kincaid always had trouble with it.

Gretel (his secretary) read me a letter from someone in the East who said, "The man who plays first flute is wonderful and I want you to tell him for me. I can hardly believe that Kincaid could be playing out there."

Just finished dinner and must work on next week's program.

Lots of love,
Elaine

Dear Mother and all,

Just came back from concert with Jose Iturbi and his sister. Iturbi gave me a bad time in rehearsals, mostly because he doesn't like women musicians—I was a little upset, but the concert went very well, and it seemed that he had dispersed all his black looks to me previously and gave them to other victims tonight. I'm glad he is not conducting here every day—a real stinker to work for.

> *Am going to doctor tomorrow to check and see if he can*
> *calm me down a little—stomach is not so good lately, either.*
> *He will probably prescribe a 2 month rest!*

New music week after week threatened Elaine's new confidence and high standard of performance. However, Maestro Ormandy assessed the concert series a complete success. He gave high praise for Elaine's work of the season and assured her she would be his first flute wherever he would conduct. She somehow felt certain this would not be in Philadelphia.

> *Hollywood Bowl Association*
> *2301 North Highland Avenue*
> *September 9, 1948*

Dear Mr. and Mrs. Shaffer,
> *Now that our season is finished, I have a heartfelt desire*
> *to write and congratulate you on the successful debut of Elaine*
> *as first flutist. I rarely make such a statement, but I dare say*
> *that, next to Kincaid, she already is one of our greatest flutists*
> *in the world.*

> *Again my congratulations,*
> *(signed) Eugene Ormandy*

Symphony Life: The Houston Symphony

The energetic Maestro Kurtz arrived in Texas to find himself in the midst of the vibrant renewal of the city of Houston. He intended to build a first-rate orchestra to complement the visible post-war prosperity.

Elaine moved among the construction bustle and clatter, reluctant to breathe its dust. Everywhere evidence of the momentum of a city caught up in urban expansion surrounded her. High rising buildings of glass and steel, the luxurious Shamrock Hotel, The Warwick Hotel, and Bonwit Tellers prepared to display the city's confident optimism, sparkling as they rose to unheard-of heights.

Elaine, along with Laila Storch, both principals in the orchestra, scoured newspapers for affordable housing. A reporter from *The Houston Post*, eager to interview the young artists, photographed them in a phone booth with the local classified section spread before them.

Municipal housing challenged the musicians as well as an inadequate concert hall or opera house, not in the future plans of the movers and shakers. The orchestra expected improved facilities on tour in the state capital, but instead played in the gymnasium of the University of Texas in Austin.

As an east coast transplant Elaine felt displaced in this foreign culture. At once, the extremes of weather exasperated her after the past season in California. She wrote:

> *The weather is enough to drive you crazy. Yesterday it was 75 degrees and humidity very high. After children's concert in the afternoon there was a terrific downpour and I was completely soaked. Then last night it went down to 48 degrees and we had to turn on the heater. Now tonight it is*

> *supposed to go below freezing. The changes are drastic and*
> *sudden. The true Houston climate is here again—82 degrees*
> *yesterday and about 100% humidity. I was dripping during*
> *the concert—then half the night up chasing mosquitoes. There*
> *were two, one in each ear!*

The Texans' lingering frontier drawl and slips of tongue and pen amused Elaine.

> *In the paper last week there was a record advertisement*
> *which included the following:*
> *D Major concerto —Zino Frances Cutti $3.85 (correct sp.*
> *Francescatti)*
> *Brahms-Strauss Waltzes $4.85*
> *Eugene Ormandy $3.85*
> *I almost wanted to send it to Ormandy, to show how*
> *much he is worth! They don't even say what orchestra or what*
> *piece—just E.O., $3.85! Tonight it said Dr. Karl Kreuger*
> *will conduct the Detroit Symphony No. 2 in D major. The*
> *announcer on one of these record programs: "You have just*
> *heard the Brahms Second Symphony under the conduction*
> *of Arturo Toscaninni." On opening night the richest man in*
> *Houston, Mr. Cullon, made a speech before the concert in*
> *which he spoke about the fine "orchestry."*

On tour in Louisiana, more local lingo from a radio disc jockey:

> *"If you want to hear this again, come down to the*
> *auditorium tomorrow night and hear Eee-frem Kurtz and*
> *his boys really kick this number around."*

More important than the folksy expressions, how would Texas audiences assess Elaine's music-making? Two opening concerts featured Ravel's *Daphnis and Chloe* and Debussy's *Afternoon of a Faun*. The Debussy piece had the familiar, beautiful solo. Her playing brought an enthusiastic response that called for two bows.

Late at night Elaine checked newsstands for the critics' reviews. What of this newcomer? Irrelevant comments were a major frustration. She was a novelty, not only as a woman musician, but as a flutist. At first, her musicality was bypassed to describe "the color of her frock," or the holding of the flute, a "musical pipe." Woodwind players were characterized as "head bobbers."

Elaine overlooked their frivolity and perhaps their limited exposure to classical music, and longed to be heard intelligently. It took some time to see it happen with a prominent journalist and music critic of *The Houston Post*.

> *(Roussel) completely ignored my solos on the first two concerts, Daphnis and Chloe and Afternoon of a Faun. I played the Faun like I've never played before and not one word in his review about me. He wrote as if Kurtz were playing the flute. I was really angry—and then the stupid woman in the other paper wrote that she thought it was nice of the conductor to give credit to the soloists in the orchestra even when they have only small passages. She said, "they take bows, too." Obviously she is talking about me, because I have been the only one to take bows. I wouldn't mind, but I would like to send reviews to Kincaid and by the way they write, it sounds like I wasn't there.*

Elaine received consolation from a sensitive, well-known Houston philanthropist and supporter:

> *Ima Hogg, the president of the Symphony, and a sweet woman, said to me after the concert when we played Afternoon of a Faun, "You took us to heaven with your playing."*

Prominent guest conductors and outstanding soloists highlighted many musical evenings in Houston. Elaine shared concerts under conductors Sir Thomas Beecham, Bruno Walter, Eugene Ormandy, Leopold Stokowski and Dimitri Mitropoulis. Soloists, Artur Rubinstein and Ania Dorfman appeared as pianists and Jascha Heifetz, as violinist. Curtis colleagues, Seymour Lipkin, pianist, and Norman Carol, violinist, were scheduled to solo. (Military duty called Norman Carol. After the war, however, he became concertmaster of the Philadelphia Orchestra.)

Collaborating with these renowned musicians from her chair in the orchestra exhilarated Elaine. A cherished comment from Artur Rubinstein lingered after her flute solo in the slow movement at the beginning of the Tchaikovsky *Concerto:* "You are a great artist."

> *I was surprised because he never talks to anyone in the orchestra. Later in the evening he asked me if I was a Kincaid pupil and said he told his wife, "She sounds just like Kincaid." Because of this inspiration and his wonderful playing I played even better in the concert. It was his 63rd birthday and his wife came to surprise him. After the concert they came to the Shamrock and stayed until 2.30 AM. I was enjoying it too much to leave—he is a fascinating person. He will be like Paderewski: a legend. Later he autographed his photograph: "to Elaine Shaffer with all my admiration for her art and cordial wishes for her career."*

That very late night in 1950 with Rubinstein and his wife only inspired her performance the next day. She played a work by Hindemith in a chamber music concert and a burst of applause surprised her.

> *I was terribly nervous until going on the stage. I wish you could have been there. You know Hindemith is very modern music, and I thought it may be <u>interesting</u> for the public. Everyone was crazy about it. Albert Hirsch played the piano and he is wonderful. Roussel must have liked it too, from his review. One word made me happy—"<u>dramatic</u>." Don't think anyone ever said that about a flute before.*

Prokofieff arrived to conduct more modern music: his own composition, *Symphony No. 6.*

> *You'll see the review—there were at least 50 people walked out. But Prokofieff himself said, "They hate what they do not understand." What we should have done is to play the whole thing through again, because it is complicated and difficult for the first hearing. I hope the same reception isn't felt when we are in Chicago. Kurtz has already phoned Cassidy (the #1 critic there) to come to the rehearsal and we will play it through twice for her. But anyway she is a*

42

much more intelligent and informed critic than any one in Houston.

Within a few seasons, Roussel wrote consistently "wonderful articles," understanding Elaine's music as he covered the classical scene in Houston. *I think he is getting in love with me; he likes the Telemann and wants to come to rehearsal.*

The Houston Symphony 1951 season's subscription concert featured Elaine as soloist. Roussel's review:

> **Miss Shaffer, the orchestra's splendid first flutist, was presented in the tremendously charming Suite No. 2 in B Minor of J. S. Bach. What she revealed was what every discriminating listener has known since she came here with Efrem Kurtz in 1948: that <u>Miss Shaffer is one of the very finest flutists to be heard in this country today.</u> Other conductors may properly envy us this interesting lady—and they do. <u>Her position in this orchestra is rather singular; she is in any case a jewel who would shine in any musical company.</u>**
>
> **Primarily, her distinction is tonal; she simply plays the flute with as round and perfectly centered a tone as it is possible to produce with consistency. It has a softness and character all its own; it is an intensely feminine sound <u>managed with a firmness which is full of masculine logic.</u>**
>
> **Along with this individuality of timbre and resonance, Miss Shaffer has a truly comprehensive and <u>splendidly flexible technique.</u> She plays with <u>virtuosic command,</u> an acute rhythmic awareness, superb phrasing and that feeling for the significant accent which is not teachable and must result from a really musicianly instinct— <u>she is an artist who performs with immaculate taste, polish and high beauty.</u>**
>
> **She is a stylist, naturally, and her musicianship has never shown to better advantage than it did in the Bach**

Suite, which is 15 minutes of steady and devilishly difficult work for the flutist. Miss Shaffer properly sat down to her task, which is sensible treatment of the diaphragm, and she played with magic lightness, spirit and freedom—especially in the Sarabande movement, the variations of the <u>Polonaise and the Presto finale.</u> They called Miss Shaffer at the end for a truly sumptuous and deserved ovation. (Elaine's underlining)

In her final season, a critic of a chamber music concert described her as **making the evening** and **one of the soundest technicians and surest artists of her instrument in the country today.**

Columbia Records agreed to record the Houston Symphony. The new challenge prepared Elaine for exacting recording some years later in London.

It is much worse than playing concerts. Somebody makes a mistake and you have to cut it over again. They had a lot of trouble with noises from the street. The engineers said it would be a fine hall to record if it were sound proofed.

Kurtz pulled a fast one today. The pieces to record have been known for a long time, but just as I came in the hall someone gave me a message to practice Pavanne by Faure, which is entirely flute solo (about 3 minutes long). We didn't have a chance to rehearse it, and they did only one "take" on it but the playback sounded pretty good. I would like to have had another chance to make it better but it may have gotten worse. It was nice of Kurtz to think of that piece for me when they needed extra time. The Columbia men were excited with the orchestra, so much so that they offered Johnson [manager] *a contract for 12 albums for next season.*

The Houston Symphony negotiated a new season, proud of their venture into recording. The Cleveland Orchestra had been dropped from recording, and Philadelphia did only two albums. Sir Thomas Beecham, visiting guest conductor, impressed with the recording outcome, dangled an offer for the orchestra to play in Edinburgh.

Tours across the southwest and on the east coast of America were lengthy and exhausting, sometimes covering 600 miles by means of bus, train or automobile.

Kurtz showcased Elaine's solos at every opportunity until she felt at times as if she had no lip.

> *The day after I return from the tour, I will be playing the Bach Brandenburg Concerto No. 2—it is for 4 solo instruments and strings, trumpet, flute, oboe and violin. Don't know where we will get the strength. It is more a test of endurance than anything else. Then I expect to play my solo (Telemann Suite) at the Pension Fund concert in the Little Theater.*
>
> *Last night's concert was an ordeal as I couldn't see the music. I nearly fell asleep in a concert in Shreveport—caught myself on the stand. It is the nearest I have come to fainting, just from lack of sleep and blowing so hard.*

Elaine's career flourished along with the young, booming city of Houston. Audience response and critiques affirmed her in solo performances and in woodwind passages scattered among orchestral works. Nevertheless, a gnawing resistance to a lifetime of rehearsals, grueling tours, new music, and the routine of an orchestra member, lacked the challenge Elaine had envisioned for her future. *"Watching the rests go by with the flute across my lap."*

High moments with solos came too seldom. Her temperament yearned for a wider venue where she could express herself more fully. She was on tiptoe, ready to give back all she felt and all she had learned, using the flute as a solo instrument.

Sensitive to Elaine's restless wonderings, Kurtz shared his own expansive ambitions. He saw a unique future for Elaine. Often the dimensions of his conversation extended to what he believed lay beyond Houston. Artists sometimes unmask their instruments and the world marvels. "You can do what Heifetz and Rubinstein have done with a solo instrument," he said. Elaine herself had begun to hear of the remarkable Segovia and what he had done, elevating the guitar to a unique classical instrument.

One evening Efrem entertained Leopold Stokowski who had conducted the Houston Symphony. Elaine prepared the late dinner at her apartment.

> *Efi asked Stoki if Kincaid is the greatest flutist in America. Stoki said, "He was, but Elaine is now. She has far surpassed him in many ways. She has some qualities which he never had."*

Another fall and winter concert season ended and Elaine headed to Los Angeles for a second summer to complete her residency so as to be eligible for jobs in the film and television industry, if not in orchestral work.

The Hollywood Bowl was out of the question that summer of 1950. Both Kincaid and Ormandy mysteriously advised against pursuing its offer for anything less than first flute. News of financial difficulties, listings of guest conductors floated about and suddenly Ormandy canceled his contract as conductor at the Bowl.

Elaine made the rounds of Columbia and RKO film studios with only an offer of a half day's work for $56.63. The Bach Festival in Carmel by the Sea wanted her as soloist but would pay only expenses. *"I would rather play that music than anything else. I'm engaged for the Bach Festival in Pennsylvania, but I'm not likely to go east for one engagement."*

The Ojai Festival under Thor Johnson of the Cincinnati Orchestra hired Elaine as second flute, with George Drexler of the Los Angeles Philharmonic as first. Johnson programmed the Hindemith *Concerto for Woodwinds* with prominent flute parts. Drexler had the music for two weeks and relinquished it to Elaine allowing her only overnight to prepare it. The performance received generous compliments from orchestra members, well worth her earlier chagrin. But the difficult times for the film and music industry left Elaine with little to supplement her income and with dim hope for a professional future in California.

European Interlude

Just as Elaine prepared to face the fall season in Houston, Maestro Kurtz returned from his summer abroad. He brought lavish descriptions of the favorable artistic climate in Europe, especially its openness to American artists. Elaine found it interesting, and even tantalizing. By the spring of 1951 the conductor and the orchestra's flutist boarded the French liner *Liberté*, as it sailed for Europe.

Disembarking in LeHavre, Elaine took in an enthralling world that Efrem knew so well. Conductor of the Ballet Russe de Monte Carlo for many years, he was familiar with the Continent's haunts. Nothing prepared her for the spectacle of Paris, the luxurious French Riviera, the bustle of Italy and the majestic Swiss Alps. Quickly her small Plymouth learned to hold to the narrow roads of the French countryside with its enchanting villages, ancient arches and quaint stone bridges.

Their itinerary introduced Elaine to Montecatini's famous health spa in Italy. At Montecatini Terme the rich and famous came for "the cure." Celebrities, Andre Kostelanez and Lily Pons, Leopold Stokowski and Gloria Vanderbilt, Goddard Leiberson and Vera Zorina, and Samuel Goldwyn, returned there. These were Efrem's friends, Russian-born or musical compatriots. At first, Elaine tolerated extravagant lifestyles, and pretentious individuals, but graciously acknowledged that underneath a hearty sense of humor and mutual musical interests she found good company.

Lily's big Cadillac is here and yet they go on trains and planes and send the car by chauffeur. They want to drive from Cannes to Italy with us (in my car). I drove the 300 miles, over winding roads and Andre talking all the time! When we arrived he wanted to go to Florence, wants to be running somewhere, and I just can't do it. I generally have such fun with him. I like Lily very much—we see them every day. Stokowski and Gloria came for dinner—she is really nice, very simple and friendlier than in Houston. The two of them talk all the time only about the children—she invited me to visit her when I go back to N.Y. Went with her to the concert Stoki conducted in Florence, the Beethoven 9th with choir.

A distinctive friend from Efrem's early life in Berlin, Herbert Israel, appeared at the spa on occasion. He was drawn to the spa and enjoyed following Efrem's and Elaine's performance schedules. Elaine spoke of the close friendship and regard for him as "a wonderful person" available to take long walks, guide her through museums and major cities he knew well, and keep her company when Efrem visited the casino. Elaine later wrote of the uniqueness of this long relationship and Herbert's sporadic visits, almost as part of her family.

London Delights

Elaine took great pleasure in London's civility and culture and in 1952 found it the highlight of their second European sojourn. On board the luxurious liner *Queen Mary*, she had a foretaste of British propriety and meticulous service. She soon learned of the city's sumptuous theatrical and musical performances.

> *The city of London is a music lover's paradise. From April to July there are concerts every night somewhere. Of course they have four symphony orchestras. Tickets are as affordable for the average citizen as a movie ticket.*

She thrilled to concerts at every opportunity and especially to the Berlin Philharmonic with Furtwangler conducting. Honored to meet him, she regretted that he would never conduct in America, accused of performing for the Nazis in his homeland. Efrem already had contacts and friends in London from years as guest conductor and from his recordings. A social evening in the home of conductor Sir Malcolm Sargent followed the performance of Haydn's *Creation* with the Royal Choral Society of 700 voices. Among the guests were Prince Georg and Princess Anne of Denmark and William Morris of the American Embassy, and Lady Mountbatten.

> *I love this country, especially London. There is something solid and enduring about it. I think it is mostly due to the strong spiritual values, and the strength of the church in this country. Also there is centuries old culture, a society of decorum and elegance, the sense of order and civilized living.*

Responsive managers finalized contracts that assured Elaine of a performance in London's Festival Hall the following year.

Leaving Europe aboard the *Saturnia*, an Italian liner, she shared reflections on her new-found world.

> *It is even better than last time. There are certain qualities here which America can never offer. It is almost impossible to be nervous, irritated or unhappy. The whole atmosphere is peaceful and contented. It is a terrible feeling to leave. The whole summer was a dream and now back to reality.*

Reality meant Houston and restiveness with negotiations between the management, the board, and the conductor. Word of financial short falls, cost cutting, positions to be eliminated, and wavering support for Kurtz unnerved Elaine. Immune to the politics, the symphony itself produced a positive message.

Other rumblings annoyed her, especially the press seeking information about her relationship to her conductor after they returned from the summer together in Europe.

> *The orchestra sounds wonderful, better than Philadelphia to me. Everyone individually seems to have improved. There is such a good spirit of cooperation and pride. It will be a shame if the board and Houston will ruin it.*
>
> *And worst of all that silly press is bothering everyone again—so far they haven't called me. I am prepared for them—the funny thing is my number is in the phone book. They call Efrem at 6.00 AM and call Laila and ask her if Efrem and I are married. I no longer go to the Shamrock. Also in the orchestra I don't ever talk to him or go in his room. Even if it isn't easy this way, I prefer it to letting some of these people get some gossip.*

The Houston season could not pass quickly enough. Elaine was lauded in Texas but now her heart was set on Europe once more. A London debut in May 1953, an immense undertaking, consumed her. She knew she would perform as a little-known American woman, a flute soloist. She did not dream of the extent of a magical evening, with a stellar performance that garnered glowing reviews and one dramatic headline that launched her European career.

Angel in Black—London Debut

" . . . and what sounds issued from that little instrument"

AMERICAN FLAUTIST WITH PIANO AND HARPSICHORD

Huge posters plastered about London's Royal Festival Hall greeted Elaine when she arrived from America on the ocean liner *Queen Mary*. *I could use it to paper my walls,* Elaine wrote. Was she, the young artist, ready to take the giant leap to "test the waters" on these shores—both as an unknown and as a woman?

According to her British manager, S. A. Gorlinsky, the public's attention was attributed to Elaine's concert being "unusual." *Like a two headed man?* quipped Elaine. *Life and Time are interested if the reviews are very bad or very good. One of them is very easy.*

This newcomer attracted reporters from several newspapers who had to first make her acquaintance and find an angle apart from music with which to describe her.

> Cecil Smith, *The London Daily Express,* May 15, 1953
> **As she talked at lunch, Elaine Shaffer might have been a fashion model on a holiday. From her finely chiseled face and rounded forehead, her hair swept straight back into a large, dramatic bun. She wore a simple frock with the poised knowledge that it is not what you wear, but how you wear it.**
>
> **The notion of becoming a model, however, never entered the comely head of this 25-year-old girl from Altoona, Pennsylvania. One task alone has absorbed her entire thought and energy. She has been making herself one of the world's best flautists.**

50

> **In a couple of concentrated years (she) has shot to
> the top of her field like an arrow . . . Tonight Elaine
> plays outside her native land for the first time. With
> Gerald Moore as her accompanist she will present a
> programme of sonatas and other sober flute solos in
> the Festival Hall Recital Room.**

Another reporter (Preston Benson, *The Star*, May 12, 1953) unearthed the "secret" to **her unusual sustained lung-power. She trains like an athlete and runs two or three miles a day to keep her breathing strength in trim.** Elaine was impatient but charming when she talked to Benson about things other than her music.

"Swimming and running are her chief non-musical activities," he wrote.

"I can stay under water 40 seconds," Elaine said.

"Is that good?" he asked.

"Not very. I am working hard to lengthen the time."

Limbering up with a toe touch before an open window made a striking pose for a news photo. Elaine was distinctive in black and white checkered pajamas. The caption: **Strenuous morning exercises, then a brisk run round the park just like a heavy-weight boxer, only Elaine Shaffer, 25, is ready to Play a Flute. Rated America's top flautist she trains to keep perfect breath control.**

The stage manager's knock on the door minutes before the performance was to her *like going to the gallows.*

Elaine performed Telemann's *Suite in A Minor for Strings and Harpsichord*. The program included Handel's *Sonata in F* (for flute and harpsichord) and Schubert's *Introduction and Variations on "Ihr Blumlein Alle"* (for flute and piano), as well as the Hindemith *Sonata* (for flute and piano).

The magic of that evening, the "unusual" concert, the astonishing performance, had critics scrambling for words. **The Princess of the Angels Plays the Flute,** a headline wired from the Associated Press, announced it **a resounding success.**

AN ANGEL IN BLACK PLAYS A FLUTE
Cecil Smith, *The Daily Express,* London, May 16, 1953

We are told that the harp is the instrument of the angels. But last night I discovered that the princess of the angels plays the flute.

In a black velvet gown with a diagonal band of embroidered white leaves, 25-year-old Elaine Shaffer looked like the subject of a painting as she tilted her head over her gleaming silver flute. Her serene Pennsylvanian face was a study in rapt concentration.

And what sounds issued from that little instrument! From the softest whisper to the most urgent fortissimo, from the most leisurely melodies to the most twinkling, rapid figurations, she made it speak exactly as she wanted it to. Every measure was deeply, movingly musical. Wanda Landowska does not play Handel more beautifully on her harpsichord. The unforgotten Schubert of Fritz Kreisler was not more ravishingly sweet.

Miss Shaffer profited from the incomparable partnership of Gerald Moore at the piano in Hindemith and Schubert works, and from the expert co-operation of Denis Vaughan at the harpsichord in 18th century music.

But the whole triumph was Elaine Shaffer's. She is one of the greatest musical performers now before the public.

The Times (London) declared Elaine's recital **the outstanding recital of the week,** commending her **sweet, clear tone . . . musicianship of the first order.** Mr. Gerald Moore was noted as **a little too robust in the Schubert.**

The Arts column in the *Sunday Times* gave brief reviews of seven recitals that week. Elaine's was one of two performances that rated positive remarks. **Her phrasing was every bit as sensitive and varied as that which can be more easily obtained from a stringed instrument.** *The Daily Telegraph* (London) noted the enthusiastic audience, and Elaine's **pure, full, impeccable phrasing, admirably displayed in Telemann's *A Minor Suite for Strings and Harpsichord.***

Elaine commented on the audience support: *The London AP man (Mr. Topping) is so sweet. He was in the audience. Many people from the American Embassy and Alicia Markova, the great ballerina, also, many flute players in the front row, breathing down my neck.*

Realistic about building her career, she would pursue and conquer opportunities one country after another. She and Efrem along with her manager reflected on the London reception and projected plans for work on the Continent. She assessed the general quality of woodwind playing *as from the Dark Ages* after attending concerts in London, Paris, Rome and Florence.

The Director of French Radio said, "No American flutist can ever be better than the French ones, because the French have the greatest flute-playing tradition in the world. In Europe they are the worst ones." Madam Bouchonet, manager in Paris, countered that there were no women flutists in France and that Elaine would have many concerts if she stayed in Paris.

An established "name," Jean-Pierre Rampal, came to mind whenever Paris was considered. He was a Frenchman with an international reputation from his recordings and appearances. Elaine made a point to hear him at a convenient opportunity, dashing to London during the Bath Festival.

Lausanne
17 May 1954

Dear Mother,

I have always heard about him and was interested. Now am more confident than ever, and am not stopping work now (as originally planned). He played so quickly, very flashy, but no content, and no style. The Telegraph *critic wrote badly, but* Times *was not too bad—though not as good as mine. There were criticisms throughout. I was always afraid to play in Paris, because of him, but now I am arranging the Bach programs there. I want to be on top, after hearing Rampal.*

Early in her career Elaine was occasionally asked if she knew this "other flutist" (flautist was used in Europe). Her gracious, brief reply, "Yes, I've heard him play."

In time a global itinerary included Paris where audiences gave enthusiastic ovations and opened its doors to this American woman.

A Catapulting Career

The headline "Angel in Black," after Elaine's successful London debut, signaled the right time to promote her in Europe. Her manager put future engagements in place and wanted to bill her as "the world's greatest flutist." After all she was new on the concert scene and unique, lacking the prestige of a child wonder or winner of a major competition. But for Elaine the important building blocks of creating a career could not be postponed.

Her own business affairs in America had to be in order, first the resignation from the Houston Symphony. Another pressing matter was a six-month residency in New York for membership in the musicians union. Elaine's dream for future success included plans for an eye-opening debut in New York City's Lincoln Center.

The lonely winter of 1953-54 in the big city found Elaine without Efrem, who was conducting the Houston Symphony in Texas for his final season. Elaine kept a rigid schedule to match the busy pace of New York. She memorized music, accepted invitations to join improvised chamber groups, and even sat with the Virtuosi di Roma Chamber Orchestra performing in New York. She enjoyed dinner and a movie with Pierre Fournier, the cellist, performing at Carnegie Hall. An ambitious recital program at the Princeton Theological Seminary was arranged by our brother, Bob, studying there for the ministry. She began biweekly French lessons at the Berlitz School and found an artistic outlet, designing her own brochures and promotional materials that her manager deemed impressive and professional.

A visit home in Pennsylvania delighted her family and she made certain to travel to Philadelphia to check in and play for Mr. Kincaid.

> He was quiet, and at last said "fine" after I played for him. Then he added that Curtis should install a monument for me because they have never produced anything to equal what I have done.

Efrem arrived to be with Elaine in New York during a break in his winter concert series in Houston. He escorted her to familiar sites about the city and introduced her to his influential friends.

> *Last night we had dinner in a wonderful restaurant in Chinatown. We were with Max Frohman, assistant to Sol Hurok (impresario). Since I met Hurok the other night he is interested in signing me as one of his artists. It is one of the impossible dreams that would be too much to expect. To be under his management would be the top of all managements of the world. Maybe you have seen the movie of his life, "Tonight We Sing."*

Excitement lingered in and about New York over Elaine's earlier triumph in London's Festival Hall. News circulated that Virgil Thomson composed a concerto for her and had asked that its first performance be at The Venice Music Festival in September 1954. Leopold Stokowski was in New York and expressed an interest in having her perform the concerto with his recording orchestra in Carnegie Hall.

Once the New York residency was fulfilled, Elaine again boarded the *Queen Mary*. Her British manager had kept her informed of a schedule of engagements waiting. Concerts in Amsterdam, The Hague, and Copenhagen launched a full European season.

Concertizing in the "cool" countries of Holland and Denmark had fresh surprises. This unfamiliar culture did not promise a warm reception. The audiences were likely to be cool to recitals, her instrument, her music, and even her unfamiliar name!

Amsterdam

> *In Amsterdam everyone said that for recitals, not more than 40 or 50 people usually go, but there were 300, nearly full house. Of course, we gave away a lot of tickets, but it's the only way, the first time. I was quite nervous, and never felt comfortable the whole evening, but played well, I thought. The reviews were generally good, but all had something to criticize. They are very <u>tough</u> in Amsterdam, and there is, I'm sure, a reason or two for this reception. 1) They don't know anything (as usual) and they discuss with each other during the concert,*

and after a "huddle" they all decide whether it was good or not. 2) During intermission, a very arrogant gentleman came to my dressing room, and said, "I'm Mr. B . . . , solo flutist of the Concertgebouw Orchestra. But don't let me make you nervous—just pretend I'm not here." It seems that he is a "big wheel" in Amsterdam, so after the concert he spoke with my manager, Mrs. Beek, telling <u>his</u> opinions and <u>then</u> all of the critics asked <u>him</u> his opinion! It really is hardly fair, and I can't imagine Kincaid doing such a thing.

Everyone says they can't understand why the reviews were not raving because Holland has never heard such flute playing. Both the pianist and harpsichordist with whom I played said that it was far above what anyone has ever done here. The curious thing is that Amsterdam and The Hague are rivals, and usually the critics are opposite in each town. Two people from the American Embassy said they couldn't understand the critics in Amsterdam. One critic attacked me for having an "Americanized" style (whatever <u>that</u> means).

Niews van de Dag, May 1954
Whether she plays a sonata by Handel or Hindemith, she displays perfect control of her instrument. The audience was enthusiastic.

The Hague

Last night I played in The Hague and I was more satisfied with the performance. The audience was extremely enthusiastic—they <u>stood up</u>. The reviews of The Hague were better than Amsterdam, but still a bit idiotic. They write only to show what they know, which is not much. And because they have never heard this type of a recital before, they have nothing to base their opinions on. The funny thing is they are contradictory: one says, not a good tone, the other, exquisite tone. One likes the program, the other wants more small pieces, etc. It would make me upset if I didn't know that I played better than ever. The manager said my reviews are much better than they usually are first time. They all say I am a great or prominent artist, but then they begin to pick about

*stupid things. Mrs. Beek says they are idiots, because she was
there, and she knows how I played, and also the tremendous
reception of the public. She is going ahead planning a tour of
Holland for next year. (I would like to play again in October
in Amsterdam, and knock them until they wake up.)*

Het Binnenhof, May 1954
**She scored ovational success—there were people who
thought her the greatest among the great.**

Copenhagen

*After many warnings that it was too late in the season,
and no one goes to recitals, there were about 150 people in
the hall, enough that it did not seem empty at all. They were
very enthusiastic, but not as excited as in Holland. I played
very well—it is such a strain, though and there are moments
during the concert when it almost seems impossible to go on.
But, I must admit, that the piece is a bit easier than the
first time—nothing can be as difficult as Prokofieff. (I am
preparing some smaller pieces, to use next year.)*

*The management here is bad. They were not even at the
concert. They sent a "representative" from their office, who
turned out to be an employee of the record shop connected
with the agency! Wilhelm Hansen Agency—they have a huge
publishing house for music; they are very wealthy, and live
in castles, so they don't care about the artists. My business is
being done here through Mrs. Beek in Holland.*

Berlingske-Tidende, May 1954
**The flawless technical treatment, the perfect breathing,
technique, the expressive phrasing and beautiful tone
at once convinced you of the quality of her art.**

Managers' Recital

A small invited audience attended a recital in London's Wigmore Hall
to showcase Elaine before prospective managers. She prepared as thoroughly
as if she were to appear before thousands. Gerald Moore, the renowned

accompanist, was an understanding partner as they rehearsed Schubert, the slow movement of Bach, and the difficult Prokofieff. Well-known in Great Britain and beyond for his sensitive understanding of accomplished musicians, he had accompanied her at the Festival Hall debut and thereafter in her career. Gerald Moore wrote in his musical autobiography *Am I Too Loud?* that Elaine, along with Elizabeth Schwartzkopf, was one of the Graces he followed onto the stage.

> *My concert with Gerald Moore went very well. There were about 20 people there, mostly my Jewish friends! But the managers, Mrs. Tillett and Mr. Hunter (director of the Edinburgh Festival) were thrilled—now I am officially under the Ibbs and Tillett Agency—she is a tremendous woman, just my type and a very honest and straight forward business woman. Also, Mr. Hunter, who is associated with her, is a wonderful man. What a difference from Gorlinsky—I am very happy for this change.*

Managers/promoters bantered freely about ambitious projects—altogether more than one artist could fulfill. Hunter wanted orchestra engagements in London, and proposed the Edinburgh Festival. Mrs. Tillett would arrange a tour of Great Britain and also Germany. BBC TV and Columbia recordings were asking for her. There was a Yugoslavian offer for the spring.

> *At the moment I am relieved to have a breathing spell before the next concerts in Switzerland. Don't know how long I could stand a regular schedule.*

The French Riviera

The south of France appealed to both Elaine and Efrem as a compatible getaway. Predictably pleasant climate and the charm of small villages with their narrow cobblestone streets revived them after a busy performance season. The sun, sea air and water rejuvenated Elaine with an established routine of long rhythmic swims in the Mediterranean that allowed her to develop and maintain her breath control.

Each year Elaine's letterheads from Cannes, Nice, Monte Carlo, Cap d'Antibes evoked a scene of the utmost in beauty and luxury. The many amenities, of course, freed her for an ideal vacation with space and time to work and relax. But from her first visit in late May 1951 the Riviera's ostentatious lifestyle never unduly impressed her. Each year Efrem favored rooms of relaxation in the beautifully adorned casinos in Monte Carlo and Cannes. Elaine tolerated an occasional visit for their fascination, but not for long, and eventually avoided the smoke-filled halls altogether. She contented herself with long sessions of practice, swimming, leisurely reading, studying the Old Testament and a new discipline of learning Italian with a tutor at the beach.

> *Old Beach Hotel*
> *Monte Carlo, Monaco*
> *July 3, 1951*

> *Dear Bev,*
> *The funniest thing is to see Dr. Lin Yutang—the Chinese philosopher, author, who wrote* The Importance of Living, *which was a best seller. Sits at roulette all day writing the numbers in a book. Has lived in Cannes for two years and told me that he has been in casino nearly every day.*

Sightings of celebrities were reported each summer. Among them were Audrey Hepburn and her husband—*we helped them with directions when we met them outside their garage.* Kirk Douglas *doesn't look great in a swim suit,* and Danny Kaye, *had fun with him, but he's somehow shy—doesn't look his age at 52—we drove him 10 miles since we were going that way—he has a wife and daughter here, but is always alone—had coffee with us one day.* Greta Garbo *was in the cabana next to us. Still beautiful in her large dark glasses—very thin.* Charles Boyer *was in view of our cabana. I saw* Bob Hope *at the beach, here with his family. There is a story that he was asked if all the children were his, or was it a picnic. His reply: they are all mine and it is no picnic!*

Marc Chagall, Russian-born painter and sculpture, became a cherished friend after their first visit in 1959. He inspired Elaine, and Chagall himself responded with appreciation on their repeated visits.

Hotel de Paris
Monte Carlo
16 July 1959

Dearest Bev and Aaron,

Recording had a depressing effect on me again. I was anything but satisfied.

We visited Marc Chagall, the famous painter, and he was in the same kind of mood, thinking all his work is bad, he can't paint, etc. It seems to me that only the very young and inexperienced have some reward in feeling themselves accomplishing something, even though it may not be true that they are.

Hotel du Cap D'Antibes
30 July 1968

Dear Mother and Daddie Rex,

I have so much to tell you. Last night I played for Chagall and his wife and their close friends Professor Nef and his wife. They have a cabana in the woods and I played there just at sunset—they were such a wonderful audience. Chagall wants to paint me playing, as a theme of Orfeo. He was asked to design the scenes for the Met. Opera for that opera—of course the famous flute solo is from that, and when I played it he got tears. He is such a marvelous person and in no way would one guess he is 81 yrs. old. It was a beautiful experience—I played for 1½ hours, all from memory, mostly Bach and Mozart. We have been out twice for dinner with them.

Hotel du Cap D'Antibes
14 July 1969

Dear Mother,

The swimming has been fine. I didn't work at all. Chagall asked me to play for him and I said I couldn't because I hadn't practiced—he said, One should always work. He works every day even here when he is supposed to be on vacation—at 82 years.

> *Hotel du Cap D'Antibes*
> *22 July 1970*

Dear Beverly,
> *Chagall came yesterday—he is 83, and working all the time. His memory is astounding and his reactions those of a young man. I am going to play for him. Have been practicing because of what he told me last year, "You must <u>always</u> work." He has a strong feeling of time being short and has so much he wants to do.*

A sudden high fever and unexplained painful symptoms interrupted an exhilarating Riviera holiday in late June 1954. Elaine spent several days in bed before a diagnosis of serious appendicitis. She insisted on a delay so that the necessary surgery could be done in Switzerland at the Cecil Clinic in Lausanne. Later they learned that one or two days' delay would have been fatal.

> *I'm thankful that God gave me the courage to make the decision to operate even when it hardly seemed urgent. The doctor told me there was the beginning of peritonitis, the appendix inflamed and infected, and also it was in the wrong place—it probably had been giving me trouble for years, as in some stomach troubles. I feel better than in five years!*

After the hospital stay, traveling to Gstaad for recuperation, resuming her work, all within a month, seemed inadequate for a complete recovery, but Elaine had permission to keep her performance date. She determined to return to St. Moritz for a second year as soloist at the Engadine Festival. She knew from past experience what lay ahead that summer.

Music Festivals in Switzerland

International artists and well-travelled tourists returned year after year for great music and idyllic ambience at Europe's summer music festivals. Elaine performed in many of them, but most regularly at favorite Swiss locales, the Engadine Festival in St. Moritz, the Menuhin Festival in Gstaad, and the Lucerne Festival. Descriptions of romantic, historic settings, the prominent guests and her own successes filled her letters. Always there was the challenge of these mountains.

In Switzerland's high altitudes the flute demanded an extreme exertion of the lungs to a degree called upon by few festival artists. Elaine mustered the lung power to perform with transforming excellence. The accomplishment ultimately became one of Elaine's greatest satisfactions even though summer after summer the toll on her health brought concerns.

The Engadine Festival

St. Moritz, high in the Alps in the Engadine Valley, was popular for its relief from oppressive heat within a fairyland setting, a premier summer getaway. Luxurious accommodations and activities centered about the Palace Hotel with its affluent clientele. Elaine and Efrem came first as tourists in 1951. Invigorating clear air, brilliant blue skies, moderate temperatures, and endless snow-capped horizons, energized Elaine after long mountain walks and hikes or climbs. The clear streams for fishing completed her perfect picture.

The Palace Hotel had a long history of attracting counts and countesses, dukes and duchesses and assorted royalty. Each year entourages returned to vacation and mingle with guests with names like Astor, Vanderbilt, and Rothschild. Elaine at first was wary of the opulent life style, but soon enjoyed casual connections with respected musicians and artists.

> *There is an influx of those who flaunt post war riches,*
> *disgusting, fat, who gather to eat caviar every night. We spent*
> *a day at the violinist Szigeti's home, visited Erica Morini,*
> *saw violist, Will Primrose with his new wife and ran into*
> *George Szell, Conductor of the Cleveland Symphony on the*
> *village street.*

She met her friend, French cellist Pierre Fournier, with whom she enjoyed playing chamber music. While in New York they had shared dinner and a movie. He arrived here as a substitute for Andres Segovia.

Favorite artists performed in sites surrounding the village and captivated Elaine, part of the audience. In a reverie, somewhat as a climber feeling the call of the mountain, Elaine determined to bring her own music of Bach and Mozart to this magical place.

Her ambition belied the serious reality of thin air at 6,000 feet. Strenuous exertion and its demands on lung power required 30% more oxygen than at sea level when doing a full recital program. Also, her physician asserted it can put a strain on the heart.

The manager of festival concerts, Pastor Schulthess, invited Elaine to perform the following summer. He promised programs to include Bach and the Telemann *Suite*, and to appear as soloist with the Stuttgart (Germany) Chamber Orchestra.

On stage at the Engadine Festival for the first time in the summer of her London debut in 1953, she stirred the usually taciturn Swiss audience until they exploded with appreciation.

August 5, 1953

Dear Mother, Dad, and Pat,

> *You should have been there—I have never seen such a*
> *demonstration for any artist. They screamed, made noises*
> *with their feet, and the whole audience stood up. I was really*
> *overwhelmed, as you can imagine. I came out six times, and*
> *they would not go home, so I had to play the last movement*
> *as an encore. They really got wild! Swiss audiences are very*
> *serious, not known to be very demonstrative—it was so*
> *surprising, the reaction and to such a "dull" music as BACH.*
> *The Pastor Schulthess said he never saw such a demonstration*
> *by the public in the whole history of the festival. He wonders*

where he will put the people for the next concert. This one was sold out with 450 people.

August 7, 1953

Dear Mother, Dad and Pat,

Never again do I expect to have such a strain as yesterday's concert. 300 people in the room, breathing in all of the oxygen. At the end of each movement I was breathing just like after running up a long flight of stairs. Then besides, I got a terrible headache from the pressure—surprising that I did not collapse on the stage. Anyway, after this, anywhere will seem easy! The pastor wants me again next year, but I must find a way to decline.

The audience was wonderful, just like the other night. The Dr. (Berry) was so nice—he opened all the windows in intermission and told the people not to smoke, as he understood the problem of breathing. The harpsichord player is wonderful and we played together just like old friends.

My room is covered with flowers—looks like a funeral, so I will go fishing, and then wash the car.

Parties in small private rooms in the hotel following concerts proved to be important gatherings for networking. Friends, celebrities, and none other than Baron Rothschild attended.

Pierre Fournier made a beautiful speech, that it was the second most musical experience of his life, besides Oistrakh (the greatest living violinist).

Invitations for tea and dinner followed quite naturally, as well as conversations anticipating a return engagement

The only thing they do not realize is that maybe I will not play at all. I may not have time to spend the necessary 3 weeks here in preparation. For vacation St. Moritz is wonderful, but to be under a strain, it wears you down more than any other place.

Elaine prepared with her usual intensity for the second season of the Engadine Festival, until the emergency appendectomy interrupted. Instead of cancelling, her recovery surprised her with renewed health. The year's festival performances had its own reward. The drama of her evening of Bach was not to be missed: the dim setting in the old church and the appearance of the German writer, Herman Hesse!

St. Moritz
August 7, 1954

Dear Mother and Dad and Pat,
I really enjoy life—also, the playing has changed, more relaxed and not such a struggle. Even at this difficult altitude it is much easier than last year.
I shall never forget playing all-Bach in the church. What an atmosphere! It is unlike any American style church— mostly stone and wooden benches, very simple. Then I had an old fashioned music stand with 4 candles attached and the harpsichord player had a lamp—no other lights—everyone said the picture was unforgettable. I have never felt such a spiritual experience in a concert before—of course for Bach it was perfect, no applause, I finished the last note and slowly blew out the candles—what an act! It was Efrem's idea and it looked like spur-of-the-moment! The setting was like a Dutch painting! I really enjoyed it!

87 Gaisbergstrasse
Saltzburg-Parsch Austria
9 August 1954

Dearest Bev, [the first concerts after surgery]
The concerts in Engadine were superb. I shall never forget the one in the church (the second concert in Samedan, the same lighting, candles, etc.). I played better than ever and it was actually <u>no strain</u> at all. Of course there was not much oxygen, but I did play it without struggle. The most important thing was how everyone was deeply <u>moved</u>, not only entertained. It's the first time that people told me how <u>inspired</u> they were, and how they will live on the experience for a long time. Erica Morini was in the audience and she

66

was very much impressed. Told me I did phrasing just as she would do. (She wrote nicely in my book.)

But the most distinguished person in the audience was the famous German writer, HERMAN HESSE. He is an old man and was brought by a friend of mine. He wrote in German, "You played as a daughter of Handel or Bach— with greatest admiration." He called me "Mein libeling." The friends told me that on the way home he commented, "We must thank God that such musicality exists." They told me he was the best friend of Romain Rolland who wrote "Jean Christophe."

Elaine kept in contact with Hesse, author of notable novels and short stories and winner of the 1946 Nobel Peace Prize for Literature, when he returned to St. Moritz each summer. She read his books and referred to their strong impression, possibly in the spiritual themes that preoccupy the heroes of his writings. His death during the summer of 1971 touched her so deeply that there were *moments when life seems to stop.*

Chur, *Der Freie Raetier,* 2 August, 1954
In view of the high altitude of the Engadine, the young flautist had more "breathing worries" than she would have had at a concert in the lowland. Therefore we must acknowledge all the more her never tiring vitality of interpretation, particularly impressive in works by Bach. Herman Hesse, a faithful visitor to Engadiner Konzertwochen, attended the concerts and said to the artist: "to be able to play Bach so beautifully one must surely be the spiritual daughter of Bach!"

Engandiner Post, St. Moritz, 10 August 1954
Quite from the outset, Elaine Shaffer captures her audience by her sensitivity of style, which she feels for the music of the baroque and rococo period, a sensitivity enlivening the most unpretentious melodic phrase and making it part of the music as a whole. Fine harmonic differentiations continually created a most plastic direction of the tone. There was no one in the

audience who was not impressed by the grace and the intensity of these melodies.

The year 1955 was significant with no musical performances, but on August 15 the marriage of Elaine and Efrem was celebrated in this favorite setting. It is detailed in its own chapter.

St. Moritz
1 August 1956

Dear Mother and Dad,

The second concert was last night. It was a full house (the last three concerts before mine were nearly empty). The first was on Sunday—the church was full, and although there was no applause, there certainly was appreciation. But immediately after that I felt beaten. Dr. Berry came and we discovered that it was that <u>wind</u> again that comes from the mountains and affects nearly everyone in some way or other. He assured me that it would go away, so I was alright for last night.

15 August 1956

Dear Mother and Dad,

We had some beautiful last days in St. Moritz and some wonderful mountain climbing and walks. We were with Erica Morini and her husband there (she is a violinist). She listened to me one day and was a great help—it was interesting talking to her as she has had a great struggle, and even with her name she has to still keep contacts, etc. So it never ends and she works terribly hard (she must be over 55 yrs.). I feel sorry for her, that she began at 3 yrs. to play violin and was already giving concerts at 7 yrs., so had no real childhood. She likes my playing very much, and says that I will have a very great career.

19 August 1956

Dear Bev,

Everyone said that my concert was the best of the season. When I speak to people who were moved by it, I feel all the suffering is worthwhile, and I will probably be talked into

*doing it again. Only 3 concerts sold out, Fournier's (cello),
Haskil's (piano), and mine. They both have tremendous
names in Europe. Clara Haskil is a terrible cripple who
plays like an angel.*

St Moritz
August 7, 1958

Dear Mother,

*These concerts are a terrible strain. The doctor helps me
a lot—there is an oxygen tank in our room! The first concert
was sold out and the second will be too, very appreciative
audiences. I think it will be the last time; it is too exhausting.
Most people don't realize what an effort it is. (I may give up
recitals and only play concertos.)*

August 17, 1958

Dear Beverly and Aaron,

*I think this was my last appearance here, as it is really too
strenuous, especially Bach's Sonata recitals in this altitude. I had
pills and oxygen in my room, and actually felt not bad but since
everything is over, not very pleasant. They were all sold out and
wonderful audiences, but they are not important here.*

*We are leaving tomorrow for Gstaad, and I'm sure I will
feel better there. Efrem said that the ballerina Pavlova never
stayed in a town after she had performed, and now I believe
it is the only way, as I have been sort of low ever since, like a
let down. Efrem gave me a new bicycle for our anniversary,
and I am planning to take some long trips with Connie
Anderson, the American friend who lives in Gstaad and loves
bike riding as much as I do. I wanted to do the trip from here
to Gstaad by bike, but was advised against going alone.*

The 1960 summer festival concluded with two sold-out concerts—"a
wonderful experience." During this season she explored another dietary
practice as part of her disciplined health-conscious life style.

Palace Hotel
St. Moritz
24 July 1960

Dear Beverly,

   Am eating only vegetarian for 10 days and feel so much better—fruit, veg., nuts, whole wheat bread for protein—have lost 10 lbs., taking wonderful syrup of iron and B-12. I told the girl in the diet shop that I am a vegetarian now, she said, "You look much better than before." And to Efi she said, "You do too." He said, "You know why? I had a big steak last night." She said, "But tomorrow you will begin to feel sick."

St. Moritz
25 July 1960

Dear Beverly and Aaron,

   Yesterday was my first concert in the 14th century church of San-Gian. Never before have I played with such ease in this altitude. It was the best of any ever given here. Since it was sold out, they turned away over 150 people. I had an oxygen tank in my hotel, so could breathe it for 10 minutes before going on.

Gstaad
19 August 1960

Dear Beverly & Aaron,

   St. Moritz was also a wonderful experience this time. The first concert was sold out, and many turned away. The second, with orchestra, was also sold-out, and when I came to the stage there was an ovation for a long time, as they couldn't applaud in the church the week before (July 25). It was really a good performance of the Telemann Suite, probably my best, and I had no feeling of strain from the altitude. I don't know whether to attribute it to the vegetarian diet or what. Have also stopped drinking wine, and drink the Kaffee Hag, instead of real coffee. I haven't missed meat in 6 weeks and I feel much better. Maybe it isn't for everyone, but I tho't I would find out for me.

   I made lots of walks, and again became in love with the Engadine. It is as near to heaven as anyone could get. One has such a sense of freedom, wondering in the woods even alone, and not worrying. Besides that, I was working out with the trampoline and it was a marvelous exercise.

Melancholy reflection, with no festival performances, pervaded the summer of 1962. She immersed herself in physical exertion to occupy these weeks. News of the death of their friend, Herbert Israel, lingered from the previous years. And now word of Herman Hesse's passing.

> *Palace Hotel*
> *St. Moritz*
> *August 7, 1962*

Dear Mother,

The first two days here were extremely painful due to memories of the past 11 summers, but after 2 days I found again that joy that was always there in the unique setting.

The same physical instructor is here and I do trampoline, gymnastics every day, plus long walks, and swimming in an icy lake! He comes at 8 every morning for an hour massage. I feel about 80 years younger than in Monte Carlo. My doctor friend from Tokyo suddenly turned up here and went on one excursion with us. He is coming to Gstaad next week to attend all the Menuhin concerts of the Festival.

We were all very sad, however, as we received news of the death of Hermann Hesse; he had just had his 85th birthday on July 2, and I sent him a telegram. It is the first year he didn't come here. Strange how life goes on when there are moments when it seems to stop, sometime for even much longer than just moments.

I am not in a very good state to write more (have already torn up 3 pages).

> *Palace Hotel*
> *St. Moritz*
> *15 August 1963*

Dear Family,

I was very busy with 3 concerts, July 18, 20, 28. They went well and everyone appreciative, but as usual a great strain. I did not take the oxygen tank and should have. The main problem is lack of air in the churches when they are full and people sitting almost on one's lap!

Today I took Efi on a nice excursion, one which I have done all on foot before, but now there is a cable car part ways. We then walked an hour to a higher point, and then 2½ hours down to starting place! It goes up almost to 10,000 feet and after he stopped worrying about breathing, being dizzy, etc., he even enjoyed it. Now he just said he wants to do something like that again tomorrow! The only unfortunate thing about these lifts is that it attracts crowds of people who otherwise wouldn't walk there, and most of them are so noisy. I wonder sometimes what the world will be like in another 10-20 years.

It was my idea to return [here] to St. Moritz after doing the Gstaad Festival August 7 and 8 as Efi is more relaxed. He wakes in the middle of the night in Gstaad to think about the next day's menu. He is shopping and cooking these days as Rosa is away till October.

We intend to leave here August 31 and go to Lucerne to hear Verdi Requiem with Karajan and Leontyne Price.

Lucerne Music Festival

The Swiss manager, Schultess, had engaged Elaine a year earlier (during the Engadine Festival) for two performances at the Lucerne Festival. She considered it as important as the Salzburg and Edinburgh Festivals. Paul Sacher conducted the Collegium Musicum of Zurich. Glowing reviews used the expression "Zauberflote" (magic flute).

Lucerne
29 August 1957

Dear Daddie Rex and Mother,

It is impossible to describe the unique atmosphere of the concerts in the outdoors. The weather has been very bad, cold and rainy here lately, but for the concert evenings it was all right, especially the second evening—that was a concert of a lifetime—I have never played like that and the whole setting had another world feeling about it.

I have become somewhat of a celebrity here—people crowded around my car when I left the concerts and I am stopped in the streets all the time for autographs. There were so many famous people here—a marvelous opportunity to have been heard by so many.

Vaterland, Lucerne, Aug 27, 1957
Elaine Shaffer was an ideal interpreter. For her, virtuosity comes as a matter of course, but poetry is her highest aim.

Basler Nachrichten, Aug. 28, 1957
Never before has the flute concerto K.313 been heard in such perfection as played by Elaine Shaffer. In her hands this instrument becomes the true Magic Flute, tender, round voluminous and of absolute purity in sound.

Claude Rostand, *Carrefour,* Paris, Sept. 11, 1957
Exceptional pure tone, graceful style, phrasing of incomparable intelligence. She is obviously among the greatest of living flautists.

Menuhin Music Festival

The Yehudi Menuhin Festival, founded in 1956 by the gifted violinist, was located in the Swiss village of Saanen, in the Bernese Oberland Mountains, near Gstaad, home to Elaine and Efrem. Villagers and favorite shopkeepers recognized Elaine dressed in blue jeans and turtle neck sweater, not in her lovely concert dress, and enjoyed a chance to chat. Her music beckoned them to the rare delight of concert attendance.

The very old Saanen church with its picturesque steeple overflowed with crowds at the well-subscribed festivals. Later, an annex accommodated the sold-out audiences attracted by the internationally known Yehudi Menuhin, a resident of Gstaad.

Elaine and Yehudi Menuhin developed a friendship earlier while they concertized and recorded in England. During the York Festival: *Yehudi Menuhin is in the room next to mine, and practiced Bach until eleven at night. It was lovely. He wanted to play duets with me, but I had to leave.*

During her initial season at the Menuhin Festival, Elaine performed with Marilyn Costello, principal harp with the Philadelphia Orchestra. Ironically, after nearly a decade of summer appearances at the Gstaad Festival, Elaine's final performance was with another dear friend and collaborator, John Solum, accomplished American flute soloist and chamber music performer.

Gstaad
9 August 1960

Dear Family,
About the Festival, it is impossible to describe what a great experience it was. It seems to be the consensus that my two concerts were the favorites of all six. Every time I go down in the village there are people stopping me on the street and in shops, etc. The weather was also bad for my first one, and I didn't feel well, and it was a marathon program under any conditions. But I did enjoy the Mozart Flute and Harp Concerto with Marilyn on Sunday with Yehudi. Marilyn had her troubles, but in the end she was delighted. She has not done this kind of chamber music much, and was used to the huge tone for the Phila. Orchestra. She changed her way of playing considerably and did a beautiful job. In this atmosphere everyone becomes selfless, mostly due to the spirit of Yehudi.
Yehudi is an angel. It is impossible to describe what kind of person he is—there is a certain spirit of love that comes from him that affects everyone. He wrote in my book last night: "To Elaine, hoping you can read my heart, as otherwise these words are quite useless. With love and admiration,"

Montreux
5 September 1961

Dear Mother,
The concerts in Gstaad were beautiful, and everyone was touched by them. I never had so many phone calls, flowers and people stopping me on the street, from all over the world. One couple from West Berlin spoke to me about what the Festival meant to them, then sent 2 dozen roses to me. It really is a unique atmosphere in that church.

*Please forgive me for not writing, but during the Festival
we were so busy and afterwards went to Zermatt for Yehudi's
concert and visited Casals briefly. (He is flourishing with his
85 years.) We came here for the concert of Skrowaszewski
(conductor of Minneapolis, with whom I played in Lisbon).*

*In Zermatt we all went up the Gornergrat on a mountain
railway—then cable car and walked on the glacier, supposed
to be the most impressive sight in the world of mountains, the
Matterhorn and all the other mountains surrounding, all
over 13,000 ft. high. We took the 6 AM train, so we saw the
sun rising and the pink glow on the peaks.*

Elaine found others in her party, including Yehudi, eager for that 6
AM sunrise trip to the mountaintop. A very personal experience, a rare
connection to the beyond, related to sustained grief over the sudden death
of their friend Herbert Israel just a month earlier.

[The letter continued.]

*I thought of how Herbert would have been overjoyed
to be there. I realized that he is now seeing beauty that we
can't even imagine, he is more alive than ever to me. No
one who has not gone through this experience can know the
wonderful strength and peace that comes and the assurance
that if we love someone he can never die. This sudden loss has
done something to me that is hard to explain in words—my
body seems dead, but the spirit is more alive and aware
than ever. It is as if there is a glimpse of eternity that one
never saw before. Particularly during my concerts, I was
completely transported to another world and was not aware
of the physical presence of the audience. Therefore there was
a complete absence of "nerves" and a feeling that someone else
was playing—I didn't feel my fingers or anything, even didn't
know I was holding the flute.*

*In Zermatt I did some good climbing, and in the woods
there are occasional tiny chapels where one is in complete
silence. Of course there is still that aching feeling, and some
emptiness, but God does give us a comforter and we realize
that <u>everything</u> is for our good. I can only be thankful for*

having had a friend like Herbert and know that it cannot come again just that way.

Gstaad

8 August 1962

Dear Mother,

If not for the festival I wouldn't stay here in August. It has an atmosphere of Coney Island. (I have two more concerts.) Gstaad is crowded, and there are so many people, it is hard to walk on the street. There is also a very bad crowd, unlike any time before, due to the presence of Elizabeth Taylor—people line up in front of her chalet and wait for hours for her to come out.

Gstaad

27 August 1962

Dearest Beverly and Aaron,

Last night was my 4th and last concert (Mozart Concerto with Yehudi conducting). Everyone says it was the best concert ever in the history of the Festival.

It is such a joy to play with Yehudi. The church was packed, people sitting on steps, standing. In fact they made a public rehearsal next morning to accommodate the overflow. When packed it seats about 1000 people. I hope some day you will be able to share this experience . . . really unique.

Some came from St. Moritz. The women came from the paper shop, stayed only a day. My doctor slept in our basement and left very early in the morning. He <u>had</u> to hear the Mozart!

Gstaad

15 August 1963

Dearest Beverly and Aaron,

We were here from Aug. 4 to 9, and the weather was very bad. My 2 concerts were alright, the second one less good, but we both couldn't stand the crowds. There were never so many people. The same problem of ventilation in the church, too; my 2 concerts were sold out, over 850 people.

Letters mentioned performances at the Menuhin Festival only in passing in 1964, and not at all in my 1965 and 1967 collection.

Monte Carlo
22 July 1966

Dear Mother,

I am playing with Yehudi conducting (Menuhin Festival) on Aug. 24. Yehudi's son Jeremy (14 yrs.old) will be soloist after my concerto the same evening. That is my only one in Gstaad this summer. Intend to come back here for awhile after that.

Gstaad
August 30, 1966

Dear Mother, Dad, and Pat,

Only a note to enclose the review of 8/24 from Gstaad— it went very well and so many people were made happy, particularly local ones who never have a chance to hear any music.

Gstaad
3 September 1968

Dear Daddie Rex and Mother,

The concerts went very well here. I used the platinum flute and everyone liked the sound. The air in the church is as bad as ever and the tho't made me more nervous than usual. The musicians were all on their best behavior and I enjoyed them all. The only problem was with Ania Dorfman (pianist) with whom I should have played and it just didn't go. I truthfully told her I couldn't play with her, and she almost died from the shock. It was hard to do, but I felt that this was not a time for compromise. She played a concerto with orchestra at the last concert, so she vindicated herself, and all ended happily???

Gstaad
21 August 1969

Dear Daddie Rex and Mother,
My concerts are over—the first with orchestra was very
difficult due to the stuffy air—the church was jammed.
Second one was better. Everyone seems to be delighted with
both of them so that's all that matters

Gstaad
30 August 1970

Dear Daddie Rex and Mother,
[This concert was sold out for a long time.]
The concert was greatly enjoyed. They started <u>applauding</u>
after Danzi. I played better than I usually do in that church.
There are so many <u>problems</u> about having to play there. I
wonder if it is worth all that nervousness. Standing outside
the door waiting to go in that hot, smelly church, I feel like
Daniel going in the lion's den.
I must have looked pretty good in the new light blue dress
from Lisbon because Diana M. [Menuhin] couldn't <u>look</u> at
me as I passed by her. She deliberately turned around to talk
to someone in the row behind her! I think she prefers it when
I play badly and look <u>nervous</u>.

The heights and depths of the Menuhin Festival are read between the
lines by the summer of 1970. Elaine continued to hold great admiration
for Yehudi Menuhin as a musician. And everywhere their concerts and
recordings of Bach and Telemann were praised.

Personal incidents compromised the close relationship they enjoyed.
As a neighbor, Mr. Menuhin took the liberty of using Le Pavillon, the
Kurtz' Gstaad chalet, for an over-flow of his house guests while Elaine and
Efrem were on tour. Elaine did not attend one of the Menuhin concerts,
possibly over a real hurt: he chose two other flutists (both of them male)
on two occasions for work in England. Meanwhile Elaine's performances
and recordings with Hephzibah Menuhin continued to be well-subscribed
and ecstatically reviewed.

Gstaad
4 September 1970

Dear Daddie Rex and Mother,

Tomorrow night at the concert Yehudi is going to receive honorary citizenship of Gstaad, also his family. We are not going. He not only doesn't live here, but he was absent for 90% of his Festival this year. They will have a deficit of $8,000 for this year's Festival, because the concerts were full only when he played. Mine (with him) had the most people of all.

Gstaad
27 August 1971

Dear Mother,

Our recital last night was a real event—everyone is excited in town. It was the best we [Elaine and Hephzibah] *have ever done, and probably the best I have ever played. All of this with a bad neck (again) plus my "off" day. The Beethoven Trio is a marvelous work and I am so glad I had the idea to play it in Phila. and N.Y. (with Sol Schoenbach as bassoon). Two nights before I did Mozart Concerto with the orchestra and it was also very good, though I can't bear the conductor of Zurich Chamber Orchestra. Yehudi was not here this week, and I wished he had been because he engaged Rampal for his festival in Windsor Castle (where the Queen is present, etc.). For this reason, I have not called him and have not gone to any of his concerts here. It's surely one of his wife's doings. Even Hephzibah is fed up with them.*

Geneva Airport
Sunday Aug. 27, 1972

Dear Daddie Rex and Mother and Pat,

I feel less tired today, but it has taken a long time to recover from the effort of last week. It was a joy to play with John Solum—we were well prepared and it went extremely well—a very special atmosphere in Gstaad (Saanen church)— the porter at Gstaad's Palace Hotel said he could have sold 50 more tickets. It was jammed. Fortunately it didn't rain and temp was cool, so not too uncomfortable inside. Prof. Hadorn (physician) was so happy, you can imagine.

Hotel du Cap d'Antibes
Antibes
1 September 1972

Dear Beverly,
  It was hard to suddenly stop after those busy weeks in Gstaad, the concerts, etc., but the Drs. said I should have a rest—I was exhausted when we got to London, but the report was good.
  It was great playing with John Solum and the Cimarosa Concerto is really GAY music, Brandenburg 4th too, so it was a true "celebration of life" concert. Everyone felt the extraordinary atmosphere in the church. It must have been somewhat the same in Austria because there shouldn't <u>ever</u> be applause in that church, and they did applaud a long time after I played. Efi says I never played greater.

The 17th Yehudi Menuhin Festival in Gstaad memorialized Elaine on Sunday, September 2, 1973 with a performance of the J. S. Bach Mass in C Minor with the Zurich Chamber Orchestra and the Zurich Concert Choir, conducted by Edmund de Stoutz.

Acclaim in Europe

Elaine had met the harsh demands of the extreme altitudes of the Swiss Alps. Now the landscape of her European itinerary reported unique challenges as well as highlights from Italy, Spain, Portugal, Scotland, Czechoslovakia, and Yugoslavia. Nothing compared to an intricate modern work composed for Elaine earlier in her career. Its new difficult tonal system called for some isolated time for her to prepare its premiere.

The Venice Music Festival

Virgil Thomson, composer and music critic for the *New York Herald Tribune,* had dedicated *Concerto for Flute* for Elaine to premier September 18, 1954. The new work needed isolation and concentration before The Venice Music Festival. A small house hidden in the woods near Saltzburg, Austria proved a perfect escape to absorb the intricacies of the concerto.

> *87 Gaisbergstrasse*
> *Saltzburg-Parsch Austria*
> *15 August 1954*
>
> *Dear Mother,*
>
> *I feel like I am bringing something to life with this new concerto of Thomson—it's sort of a new sensation creating something that has never been heard before. But it is killing me—so difficult and me without any technique! He has sent the score to Ormandy who is delighted with it and wants Kincaid to play it in 1955-56. However, I have the rights to do the 1st American performance, also recording rights. I want to see how it goes in Venice—the way I feel about it now, it's worth one consecutive performance!*

August 20, 1954

Dear Bev and Aaron,

Virgil Thomson was here for 3 days and we worked hard—I was glad when he left, because every time he looked over the concerto he kept changing things! But I'm even beginning to like the piece! We became good friends too, which is important. When I took him and his boyfriend, an American painter, to the station, he kissed me and said "Goodbye, sweetie."

Now I am working 5-6 hours a day to memorize it—it is 15 minutes long—and 12-tone system so nothing related to anything else—probably like learning Greek. Nothing can get in the way or it obliterates the 12-tone wrinkles in the brain!

Virgil is going to be there for the concert and I'm glad so he can tell the conductor what to do! It is so modern and doesn't make sense, very difficult to remember. It certainly doesn't have any <u>tunes</u> to whistle on the way home!

The Vienna Festival lured Elaine and Efrem to some performances held a short distance from their woodland cottage. Furtwangler's rehearsals and the final concert with the Berlin Philharmonic were unforgettable. This conductor, considered to be the greatest, inspired both Elaine and Efi. *I never heard such an ovation! He spoke to Efrem about music in America. "One must be religious to make music. They are machines." (He meant Toscanini of course).*

Elaine and Efrem invited select guests to join them for lunch or tea at the little house. Their friend and respected conductor, Dimitri Mitropoulos, asked to come because *he hated eating in restaurants and remembered how Efrem cooked in Houston.*

15 August 1954

Dear Mother,

Mitropoulos came to our house for lunch, and ate like a horse—and he is so thin! He is sweet, and a sad kind of man—I always feel that he is completely detached from the world, and that he feels alone. Efi goes to his rehearsals and says he is absolutely a genius in modern music. But for classics he doesn't know what to do because it is difficult for him to do uncomplicated works. The orchestra loves him and also the management of the Festspiel.

Mitropoulos is interested and wants to see the Thomson score (he implied that he would like me to play it with N.Y. Philharmonic—American premiere but I suppose Wummer (first flute) would not allow it).

We had the maid make weiner-schnitzel and arrange the table. I can see that to have a house means having guests all the time.

I took M. home and went to Virgil Thomson, worked with him 3 hours (also 2 hrs. in the morning). I drove him and his boyfriend to the lakes for tea and pastry. So it was a busy day. I am happy with Virgil—he is nice to work with, and likes me.

Sept. 2, 1954

Nathan Milstein, the violinist, came to tea and I played for him for over an hour. He was much impressed and gave me some criticisms which were extremely helpful. He is a lot of fun and a very clever man, also a great musician. He gave me honest criticism which is so rare. Generally he felt that I give too much all the time, and if intense it is not impressive as it is in only certain moments of music.

Saltzburg, and the serenity and isolation of the Austrian woods, faded with the impending premier. Crossing the Italian border, approaching Venice, contrasts were striking—cheerful, friendly Italians and sun-filled days.

Elaine and Efrem indulged themselves as tourists in Venice before the composer arrived for rehearsals. Their lovely hotel overlooked the bay in Lido where there were beaches for swimming or memorable evenings sitting in St. Mark's Square.

Excelsior Palace Hotel
9 Sept. 1954

Dearest Bev,

I have a lovely room and can see Venice from here.

I work from 9-12 then go on the beach till 4.00— drink coffee, and then work again 4.30 till 7.30—sit in the

Square—so unbelievably beautiful in the moonlight. The gondolas go by with people playing accordions and singing— very romantic!

Virgil Thomson came swimming. Afterwards I played the concerto for him. He is pleased. There will be 5 rehearsals.

*Venice, Italy
18 Sept. 1954*

Dear Mother and Dad,

Well, my Italian debut was a great success—for once I am delighted with the way it went, especially since I had doubts as to whether I could play the thing, and whether it would have any response from the public. I played the best yet, with the Lord making the music.

What a hall! It is a dream, shaped like a horseshoe, with gilt-edged boxes from top gallery to the bottom, everyone in evening dress.

Last week we attended concerts and saw how cool the audience is and I feared for Virgil's opus. But they really screamed, and yelled BIS [Encore]! Everyone says it was the biggest success of the <u>whole</u> Festival—and that the composition was by far the best.

The biggest paper in Italy (Milan) wrote that I was the "outstanding" one on the program, and "exceptional artist," "young and acrobatic," and also mentioned that I had the most applause. Virgil was very happy of course. He left for New York immediately. Look for his article on Sunday.

A composer from Philadelphia (who had heard Kincaid his whole life) said it was the greatest flute playing he ever heard. There were many celebrities there in the music world, so you can see how happy I am that it went so well, since it was so important.

The orchestra was so <u>nice</u> and friendly to me—these Italians are the greatest—at each rehearsal they applauded and came to talk—they really played magnificently, and it was such a <u>good</u> feeling to have 80 admiring, handsome men on the stage with me! The conductor didn't arrive until the day before the concert, so I had 3 rehearsals with Virgil conducting—the orchestra knew the piece backwards, so they

*played for me as the conductor didn't know the piece well. I
came out 4 times which is really unheard of, especially here
for these modern music concerts.*

*Immediately after intermission I started to play—at 11
p.m. Someone said the audience was bored until I came, then
they woke up.*

The London Times, September 18, 1954
**Elaine Shaffer did some remarkable things with
attack, tonguing and staccato in the rhapsodic first
movement, in effect a huge solo cadenza, in which
the orchestra was silent, and in the gay and chirping
finale.**

L'Unita, Rome, September 18, 1954
**The highlight of the concert was the brilliant playing
of the young American flautist, Elaine Shaffer, which
displayed to full advantage her excellent technique,
and masterly breath control.**

Virgil Thomson, prolific correspondent, mentioned *Flute Concerto*
in his book Selected Letters. It included a letter to Manuel Rosenthal, a
French composer and conductor, and a personal letter to Elaine.

November 16, 1954

Cher Manuel,

[He refers first to a fine concert the night before by
Leontyne Price singing Rosenthal's early songs—and
charmingly.]

*I had intended writing you earlier about my Flute
Concerto which had its premiere in Venice on September
18th. The piece seems to be perfectly successful, and my
soloist, Elaine Shaffer, is quite a wonderful artist. She had
asked me at the time if I cared to speak about her to Henry
Barraud (French Composer, music director of the French
National Radio from 1948-1965). But I told her I preferred
not to recommend artists to Barraud, since he so easily
feels embarrassed in such a situation if he cannot use them*

immediately. If you care to pass on to Barraud or anybody else my admiration for the technique and musicianship (plus utterly charming platform presence) of Miss Shaffer, who is having considerable success as a soloist, I should be grateful. If you would care to use her in any of your own programs, with or without my concerto, I don't think you would find her disappointing.

June 8, 1956

Dear Elaine,

Our Flute Concerto has had a good season. Everywhere the public reception was enthusiastic, and everywhere but New York the press was fine too. Here the press was very poor. Everybody seemed to think it a negligible work. My theory is that none of them could listen to a quiet piece by April. Anyway, it will be played some more next year. And I am hoping that you will be able to record it sometime somewhere. Meanwhile affection to you both and all good wishes,

In the same volume in a "Letter to a Friend," Virgil Thomson, himself a critic, wrote, "Reviewers' opinions, after all, do not have to be right, they only have to be clearly expressed and reasonably defensible."

Madrid

Madrid was Andres Segovia's city. The classical guitarist made his name in Madrid producing mesmerizing music with this unlikely instrument. Elaine was in awe of his sounds, his interpretations, and his astonishing accomplishments.

Elaine accepted the challenge to play in Segovia's city, aware of the blatant barrier of her gender. By this date she is not only the soloist but the wife of Efrem Kurtz, invited to conduct the Madrid National Orchestra. A lukewarm reception is likely: *They wrote and said they were reluctant to engage a woman, especially a wife. They are still in the Dark Ages in that respect—the only country in Europe that way.*

Palace Hotel
Madrid
4 March 1956

Dearest Mother and Dad,

 The audience was screaming. One paper said that I have created a new world of my own, and as a "diva" of the flute, can be compared only with Segovia. Since Segovia is Spanish, he is an idol here; for the press to write that in Madrid is especially significant. The agent said that no artist has got such an ovation this season. I think it sounds so funny but I read that I had a "clamoroso triunfo."

A tour of the city of Toledo and a rewarding visit to the Prado Museum, took in the paintings of El Greco, Velasquez and Goya, and helped pass the time while the artists wait for news reviews. Elaine favored these Spanish masters from reading biographies that she recommended. At last the press headlines: **Exultant performances of Brahms and the Mozart Concerto open a fresh consideration of the woman as artist.**

Efrem penned his postscript:

MY ANGEL WAS AN ANGEL, FOR A SHORT TIME A DIVA—NOW THEY CALL HER HERE GODDESS— WHAT YOU THINK SHOULD I CALL HER? CAN'T SAY MY LOVE, AS NOT DIGNIFIED—AS NO ONE KNOWS THAT SHE IS MRS. EFREM KURTZ. TO BE SERIOUS SHE IS REALLY GREAT.

Germany

Tears came easily during two moving Mozart concertos performed by noted pianist, Clifford Curzon. Elaine attended his 1956 concert in London that celebrated the birth of Mozart. Afterwards she expressed to him her emotional response to his music. Curzon turned the conversation to Berlin, her recent appearance there, and that in Germany, their manager, Fineman, talked constantly of her success. Grateful for openings in Germany, a new country in her collection, her career and world was expanding.

Fineman reached her soon after she settled in with Efrem, who had been engaged to conduct the Liverpool Philharmonic for the 1955-56 season. Recitals he offered in Hamburg and Berlin took Elaine away from Liverpool in December 1955.

The German manager induced her first with prospects of playing Bach with the Stuttgart Orchestra in Berlin. She was reluctant to be apart from her husband so soon after their summer wedding. He would be alone spending a dreary fall and winter in England's fog-locked city, in their cold, damp apartment, without central heating. And yet, Berlin was hardly a warm destination for a winter holiday. Her first invitation to appear in the city of legendary, discriminating music lovers was one she could not turn away.

Once in Berlin, a rare experience confirmed her decision to come to Germany. The war-weary country, with its centers of culture, hungered for memorable music. The audience for her Bach recital called for three encores. Critics' reviews carried headlines that read **Perfect Musicianship.** In translation: **this concert brought them back at last to the joy of their profession. Critics usually go to criticize but this one had nothing to criticize.**

> *Parc Hotel, Reuteler*
> *Gstaad (B.O.) Switzerland*
> *Dec. 19, 1955*

> *Dear Mother,*
> *Both recitals (Hamburg and Berlin) went very well. The public was very enthusiastic and seemed to have a real understanding and appreciation for Bach which I have never done anywhere. I was glad to go with John Hunt, a wonderful person, besides playing well. The critics' reviews were all very good, especially the one in Berlin. I have good hopes of future concerts already promised—one in 1956-57 season with Hamburg Radio Orchestra.*

Outside the concert hall Elaine found graphic reminders of recent history in Berlin and Hamburg.

> *Berlin is such a shambles. I never realized any place could be so destroyed. I went to see the house where Efrem used to live and the whole block is empty, as are many stretches. There has been much rebuilding, but still it is shocking to see it. The people seem more on edge there too, as they well can be with those Russians on their necks.*

Cologne expressed jubilation and renewed her engagement. In fact, the reviews are, to Elaine, the greatest she has ever read about any artist! Dubbed **The American Magic Flutist** in a lengthy review, it declared **that flute playing was born with her performance, that it was a revelation.** Understandably, she was booked to return for the opening of the MEISTERSERIES. This concert series traditionally presented top names like Oistrakh in its six concerts and seldom repeated artists a second year.

> *Two rave reviews announced the very important flutist and one mentions the sensation I made last year with the Stuttgart Orchestra and the reason I was chosen to open the series. I never expected them to write like this.*

Meanwhile, Mr. Fineman worked on her behalf, responding to her successes. *He is selling me everywhere. I can't believe that such a wonderful person exists. He is a musician too and will not take any artist unless he is absolutely sold. He has such convictions and honesty. The other agents are business people and nothing else. He has many concerts for me next year.*
Her ambitious German manager arranged a 3-week tour in various venues. Munich, on December 19, 1956 was the most highly anticipated. Efrem debated joining Elaine rather than face a lonely Christmas in Liverpool. He hesitated, having fled Germany in 1933. *It is near the border and if they don't like my nose, I can always leave.* However in Munich, he found more kindness than he could have imagined. But bad memories made him eager to get away after Elaine recounted tales of the attitudes of conductors and other musicians in her tour in Germany. *They are so conceited and think they know everything. It is especially difficult for me, as even in their orchestras they have no women, so to have as soloist a flute, is too much for them to take.*

> Park Hotel
> 28 Dec. 1956

Dear Mother and Daddie Rex,
*   I wrote about Bad Godesburg where there was a rehearsal from 2-4 and a concert in the evening with two concertos. After that I continued working 8-10 hours a day for Munich. The Munich ones were on my mind due to the importance of the city, the orchestra, and the fact that it was the first time for me to do a new Mozart. Efrem came the morning of the first rehearsal. The conductor was really insulting to*

me, which didn't help. Next day he was nicer, when he saw I would not take it and in the end he was even pleased.

I don't remember any time in my life when I was more nervous, almost hysterical before a concert. At the last moment I couldn't remember anything, and took music on the stage. The following night was a repeat; then I was not so nervous, but tired, so it was also not a pleasure.

So far I have seen only one line about my Mozart, not bad, but not anything special. A terrific one from Bad Godesberg with big headlines.

Journal Notes

Dusseldorf LeClair Concerto, with orchestra. Critics say "unsurpassable," and the first time I ever played it—re-engaged immediately for spring.

Bad Godesberg (near Bonn) Bach Suite and Mozart Concerto No. 1. Spent tedious hours marking orchestra parts for both Mozart Concertos to save time in rehearsal.

Munich Mozart D Major Concerto with Munich Philharmoniker Orchestra. Terrific reviews after working hard 8-10 hours to prepare, was almost hysterical before concert.

Frankfurt Radio Orchestra. Mozart and Bach went well, unusually pleasant to do. It was a rebuke to my anti-German attitude, as I have met some wonderful people.

I am so sick of the flute and the whole profession at this point that I couldn't care less. It hardly seems worthwhile to put so much importance on something that is really not important enough to get so keyed up, and then let down afterwards. Just spoke with Bela Siki yesterday, a Hungarian pianist with whom I am doing a joint recital in London in April, and he said he can't stand the piano or music since he returned last week from a tour in Holland. I suppose it is normal, and because I ain't got no blood, (85% and anemic), I am probably more pessimistic than usual.

The entire winter tour was debilitating. Exhaustion, depression, disinterest in her profession and her instrument, overcame her, a period described as her "slough of despond." Her spirits lifted with some good work, an affirming review, or a pleasant happening such as the delivery of her Powell gold flute, on order for a year. *It is just like having a Stradivarius. I still haven't found one that plays itself.*

York Festival, with Gerald Moore

The English festival engaged Elaine to perform a Bach solo. She had hoped to cancel when it interfered with a flight to Australia with Efrem to begin their six-week tour. Instead she found herself booked in an inadequate hotel that lacked service to press her gown. The local taxi driver, with a mind of his own, delivered her to the wrong church, reasoning, "But I took a singer there!" Mrs. Tillett, her manager, never appeared. That morning concert somehow proved "deeply satisfying" to Elaine and the important *Manchester Guardian* filed a complimentary review.

> *We* [Gerald Moore, accompanist] *had our concert at 11 AM—one of the most satisfying concerts I have ever experienced—was completely transported, and I think the audience was too—it was as if someone else was playing and I was listening. There was such a mystical atmosphere from the first note and I played 1½ hours without intermission and was not even tired. There was no applause and such complete concentration that no one moved during the whole morning. Bach is marvelous in a church, especially such a beautiful old one like that.*
>
> *There were 700 people there, every seat taken. It is a concert like that that makes it seem worthwhile to blow that silly pipe.*

Granada Music Festival

> *Grand Hotel e Le Pace*
> *Montecatini Terme*
> *4 June 1958*
>
> *Dearest Beverly,*
> *I am looking forward to Granada Festival. Rubinstein and Segovia are also there. It is an exquisitely beautiful place as well as marvelous setting for concerts, mostly in courtyards of palaces.*

Gstaad
8th July 1958

Dear Mother and Dad,
    The concert in Granada was a success; the papers wrote better than I deserved, such as "triumph" etc. I hate out-of-door places, and this was a very large place, very beautiful to look at, but the acoustics were weird, and I was rather depressed afterwards. It was nice for the public, as it was a full moon and starry night. But those Spanish hours kill me, I played at midnight; the concert began at 11.15. That plus the late nights three day before made me feel as if I were sleepwalking. We finished the concert at 2.30 and then sat with the conductor until 3.30, packed our luggage, and had an hour's sleep before leaving for Madrid.
    We were with Segovia a lot. He was playing there for the 50ᵗʰ year. He is a darling—he wants to play with me next time in Granada. Will send you a picture of us together.
    Spent time with Gerald Moore. He is such a fun person. Says something funny every minute!

Belgrade and Ljubljana

"How seldom it happens, a fabulous concert" Elaine appraised a radio broadcast of herself from Belgrade in 1958. This first visit to Yugoslavia impressed her with its destitute government. *We walked on the street today, and the people all look hungry and sad. From speaking with some, they feel fortunate when they compare themselves with Russia, Rumania, Bulgaria, etc. There are very few cars on the street—Fiat made here, which costs $1200 in Italy, costs here $10,000. They have "freedom" to leave when they wish, but are allowed to take only $10 a year out of the country.* Elaine witnessed women on the street removing snow without wearing gloves or a coat and were probably sheltered in unheated houses.

Ljubljana, Yugoslavia
January 21, 1958

Dearest Daddie Rex & Mother,
    You would not have believed your ears and eyes if you had been in Belgrade last night. Such a wonderful reception I never imagined, even though everyone told

us how extraordinarily enthusiastic the public is in this country. I must say that I played well (the first concert I have been somewhat satisfied with for a <u>long</u> time)—the audience screamed from the end of the concerto until I had nine bows—there was nothing to do but repeat the last movement of Mozart, something which happens only once in ten years, they said. The critic came backstage "to see if I was really a human being, not something from another world." It is impossible to describe in words the tremendous concentration and the "living" of each note which one feels from the audience—they are absolutely spell-bound. Last night they screamed even after the overture.

My Mozart was before intermission—then came Shostakovich's Fifth Symphony, a powerful work—Efi came out 11 times and they were absolutely wild—he would still be there if he hadn't stopped them by thanking them (in 4 languages). We will never forget the exciting evening.

Our trip here was paid both ways. We are paid in Yugoslav dinars and are allowed to take only ½ out of the country. I went out today looking for things to buy but there isn't much of quality. Incidentally I received a very low fee this time, but yesterday the agent said I can have any fee I ask next time.

They want us again already in August for the Festival at Dubrovnik, on the Adriatic, supposed to be one of the most beautiful places in the world, with 10 natural outdoor theaters. I always wanted to go there.

Elaine returned in 1960 to accompany Efrem, not expecting to perform. Conditions had improved in Yugoslavia, but still she found it a depressing place to be alone.

Belgrade
9 January 1961

Dear Mother & Daddie Rex,
When we arrived here, I discovered that they expected me to be soloist in Zagreb on Jan. 25—so that is good I didn't decide to stay in Gstaad! I am glad to play there as we have never been there, and it is the city with the best orchestra.

We came back to our hotel this eve to find the street lined with people. It is a reception for 2000 people with Tito, for one of the African leaders. There are police everywhere in the hotel—we had to come in a special entrance. We had lunch with the U.S. cultural attaché and he said if Eisenhower would come here they would make a reception, but nothing as big as this one for the Africans.

There is a big radio in our room, but we can only get one station, Belgrade. I brought a little Zenith pocket radio and we hear the most incredible propaganda from Radio Moscow, in all languages, including English. It really makes one's blood boil to listen to it. These Embassy people really have a big and important job to do in countries like this, to offset that vicious propaganda.

Conditions in general are better than last year—radio, television, appliances etc. to sell, but not many can afford to buy them—they are opening a Fiat factory soon here. There are many more cars than last year.

This hotel is very comfortable and we have a nice suite (only the light bulbs are weak—15 watts). We have two rooms—there is no heat in the radiators, but the entrance foyer is hot, and the bathroom. They gave us one little electric heater, but not two, as that would burn out the fuses.

We brought a suitcase full of food and have gone in the restaurant only for lunch. We make rose hip tea in the morning, and whole wheat bread, brown sugar, honey and cheese. Also fruit from Zurich.

We enjoy being with the people—they are contented with little and their minds are not full of thoughts of material things. They can afford to be that way, because they are secure for their whole lives, pensioned, sick pay, etc.

All for now. (The soldier is still walking back and forth outside in the hall. Maybe he thinks we are spies.)

Ljubliana, Yugoslavia
21 January 1961

Dear Mother,

Efi has been sick for 4 days, and even the day before he was to conduct. It was sold out in 2 hours and the people were so looking forward to it, he pulled himself together—it was a magnificent Mozart Requiem. You should see how they get wild here when they see Efi—he is really an idol in this country.

One sees some of the inadequacies of the form of government when sickness happens—no doctor would come, so he went twice in the clinic, with 100 degrees temp. Finally we got a doctor to come, and after giving him some dinars in an envelope the first time, he comes back regularly. Karl Marx couldn't change human nature!

Zagreb was postponed (we will leave tomorrow) but we can do it in 3 instead of 6 rehearsals. I can rehearse the orchestra with my Mozart, and Efi has only to do Beethoven Fifth Symphony and a small Bach Chorale.

27 January 1961

Dear Mother,

We were so <u>happy</u> to leave Yugoslavia—though the last concert in Zagreb was a huge success. I had about 9 bows and had to play an encore. Efrem was so weak and nervous he <u>fought</u> with everyone there, but they were impossible, and lied all the time—one aggravation after another. But we feel the whole tour was worthwhile if only for the <u>New York Times</u> article. Even though there are so many good things about their government, one still feels the lack of freedom. But compared with the real Communist countries, Yugoslavia is a paradise. They call themselves Socialists, but there were only a few that we met who were party members.

One man and wife had been rather well-off and everything was taken away—now they have to pay <u>rent</u> to live in their own house. He wants to have his children well educated, as he says that can't be taken away from them and money means nothing because he had it, and now he has nothing.

31 January 1961

Dear Mother,

In Zagreb we had programmed a Bach Chorale, and the words included "Oh, God, etc." They said they could not print "God" in the programme. But still they were doing the Missa Solemnis and Mozart Requiem in the same country.

You would have thought Efi was a Christian missionary to the Communists the way he talked to the choirs in Yugoslavia (in Missa Solemnis and Mozart Requiem). He said, "You don't believe what you are singing." They were singing "Christe." He said, "Lift your heads up. He is not under the earth, dead. He is alive." Both of those works were a wonderful experience.

Gulbekian Festival

Grand Hotel e La Pace
Montecatini Terme
2 July 1961

Dearest Beverly and Aaron,

The concerts in Portugal were very successful—thanks for your thoughts on those days. In Lisbon there were 3500 people and they are mad about music—I played 2 encores. The conductor, Skrowaczewski, (from Minneapolis) was good and we got along well together. He told Efi he <u>learned</u> so much from me about Mozart! (?) He asked me to Minneapolis in 1962-63 season. We were with him and his wife after the concert until 3.30 AM—next day drove to Evora (3 hrs.) for the second concert—couldn't sleep at all, and played that evening—another dinner after the concert and drove back to Lisbon—next day plane to Paris, night train to Lausanne, arriving 7 AM—errands to do, then driving here for 2 days. Still have not quite recovered.

Mrs. Joseph Kennedy was here when we arrived (Montecatini spa) and sat at the next table in dining room— she looks well preserved for her age, and everyone liked her, because she is simple and friendly with employees, etc. Also Italians were impressed that she didn't have bodyguards, police, etc.

Next stop is Hotel de Paris, Monte Carlo. How long we stay there depends on the heat—I long for the mountains, but Efi seems to enjoy being hot. Have made several excursions to Lucca, an extremely interesting historic city—one could spend a life-time in this country and never see everything.

Bath Music Festival

In the presence of Royalty and the Bishop of Bath, precedent was broken when the English bishop could not resist leading the audience in applause.

20 June 1962

Dearest Beverly and Aaron,

It was quite exciting in Bath, and at both concerts. I played above my usual standard, in fact, I was almost pleased. Is that a danger signal?? Princess Margaret and Tony came to the Bath Abbey concert where Yehudi conducted my Mozart Concerto. A precedent was set when the Bishop of Bath and Wells, sitting with the princess, couldn't refrain from applauding after my performance. (Yehudi played just before me on the program and they didn't applaud then!) London Times wrote headline "ENTHUSIASM BREAKS A CONVENTION"—then after explaining about the applause they write: "It was Miss E. Shaffer's gloriously concentrated and intensely musical playing of Mozart's G Major Flute Concerto which understandably prompted this display of enthusiasm."

It was so inspiring playing in the Abbey—it has good acoustics too. There is a picture (with the clippings) of my being presented to Princess M. and Tony. They look nice together—she is much shorter than she seemed on photos.

It was 5 days of intense work, but I am glad it went well as I needed a lift for my confidence just then.

The Queen Mother's Social Calendar, as announced in London's "Court Circular," noted her day's schedule. This day it included Elaine whose desire always had been to play before royalty.

Queen Elizabeth the Queen Mother attended a lunchtime concert in the Guildhall of St. George Kings Lynn and heard a recital by Elaine Shaffer (flute) and Gerald Moore (piano).

Le Pavillon
Gstaad
January 12, 1958

Dearest Beverly and Aaron,

The Queen Mother was so charming and easy to speak with. She spoke with me about 10 min., asking intelligent questions and even took off her glove and touched the flute! She seemed to enjoy the concert, said it was "<u>glorious</u>." She was sitting almost on my lap so I was a bit uncomfortable playing, but the experience was exciting and something that only happens once. I had practiced my curtsey, it wasn't too difficult to do, at the beginning and end of concert, then at the presentation.

It suddenly came to me that I had that ambition in younger years (probably from reading of artists like Kreisler and Rubinstein) to play for royalty, also to play in every country in the world! The biggest ambition was to make people <u>cry</u> at my concerts. Funny how these things came back to me recently, when I had almost forgotten about them.

Naples

Gstaad
11 October 1962

Dear Daddie Rex and Mother,

Monday we go to Naples to begin rehearsals for our concert where I play the Ibert Concerto for the <u>first</u> time. (Bill Kincaid always considered it too difficult, and I did too.) They played a record of his on Zurich radio last week, but not good pieces. It all depends now on my nerves at the moment of the concert, so if you could remember me at about 1.30 your time Oct. 19th, Friday, I will appreciate it. On the 20th we fly to Palermo where I do the Mozart with Efi, which will seem like a children's piece after the Ibert!!

It has been wonderful weather here most of the time, and I have made some marvelous excursions, some alone, some with Connie Anderson. I went with her up to a hut built by the Alpine Club—8,000 ft, and one has a view over all the Alps. We drove about 15 min. from Saanen and then climbed about 2 hrs.—rather steep. It is always open, and there is a box there to leave your money, (50 cents) if you stay overnight. There are so many places to be seen around here, it would take a lifetime. I am just thankful to have the luxury of time, freedom and physical health to be able to do it. Those things one couldn't buy with all the money in the world. One day when I climbed 2 hrs. and walked down 3 hrs., sort of a circle, I was so exhilarated, couldn't sleep.

Villa Igiea
Palermo, Sicily
22 October 1962

Dear Daddie Rex and Mother,
This morning's mail brought your nice birthday card—perfect timing.

My ordeal in Naples was over on Friday night with <u>huge</u> success—all the papers write "triumph." Until the last minute I was shaking and feeling sick in the stomach, headache, etc.—only nerves. From the first note, control came from <u>somewhere</u> and I didn't worry any more. It is a big <u>satisfaction</u> to have done it, something I was always afraid of—it has a million notes, and each one has a sharp or flat in front of it—it has its depth too, not only showy, a wonderful effect. I hope to record this as there is no record in existence.

Efi had a triumph too with his Beethoven <u>Eroica</u>. They really like us in San Carlo—we are already there 7 or 8 years in a row. The theater is beautiful—like La Scala, but bigger.

Vienna Concert Series and Festival

The auspicious Vienna Festival was only a dream in 1962 when Elaine first breathed the air of that city in Austria known as a center of the arts, especially music. Composers Beethoven, Mozart, and Brahms lived there. The first of a series of three concerts (not yet part of the festival) brought on

99

palpable anxiety. Just before she entered the stage the perceptive manager whispered, "You are invited to play in the festival next year!" It worked!

Gstaad

12 October 1963

Efi took me to the Musikverein, just beside the hotel, to practice and to meet Prof. Gamsjaeger who runs the whole thing. Brahms founded the M. and the professor showed me the stairs where he and Bruckner walked. The hall is a GEM, the greatest acoustics in the whole world (2100 seats). The feeling of tradition cannot be missed.

At the first rehearsal I was shocked to discover the orchestra was playing at a pitch almost a quarter of a tone higher than mine, and I couldn't do anything about it except cut a piece of the flute off! They were very nice though, and I gave my tuning fork to the oboe who made them all go down. They were impossible; I had heard about their pitch but I didn't realize it was so high.

Thursday was the first concert, and the worst day for me. The manager understood, as his wife is a singer. He said, "Pretend you have already played, and now you are going out to do it again." The audience was young, from 18-25, and they were wonderful. The next night were working people from factories (dressed and behaved like Royalty)! The third night was the one that counted; the first subscription concert for regular members of the Friends of Music of Vienna, more aware that Mozart lived in Vienna, Schubert was born and lived there, etc. Also, the critics came that night. It was a tremendous reception by the audience, screaming, and each of us had 5 or 6 bows.

For me, it was one of those RARE performances (like last year returning to Kansas City) where time and place seemed to disappear, and I could transmit a message that had nothing to do with me, and I felt I was a listener.

The day after the first reviews appeared Mrs. Van Karajan came to the first half of the concert, probably to check up on me. Her husband was conducting the same night at the opera.

Segovia was also in town, and came one evening to
hear us. He wants to do something with me as he was very
enthusiastic, but there is so little music for flute and guitar.
We are both trying to commission a good work.

The Vienna Festival the following year announced an extraordinary event—the appearance of David Oistrakh, the outstanding Russian violinist, highly admired by Elaine, as conductor for her solos. She prepared the modern works of Ibert and Ghedini and then heard the shocking news of Oistrakh's heart attack. This meant the cancellation of his program. Word came that his son, Igor, would conduct instead. Igor, a violinist like his father, had never conducted.

Imperial Hotel
Vienna, Austria
8 June 1964
Dear Daddie Rex and Mother,
Yesterday morning we had the first concert. Igor Oistrakh
played 2 concertos and I did the Flute and Harp Concerto.
Efrem was persuaded to conduct at the last moment as Igor
couldn't do it. The place was sold out, even 150 people on the
stage. Tremendous success—the Prof. Gamsjaeger said it was
the best concert of the festival so far.

Gstaad
25 June 1964
Dear Daddie Rex and Mother,
The last two concerts were murder for me. The Ibert
Concerto was again a traumatic shock—I was in knots and
had a terrible headache for 2 days after. One hour before the
concert I went to pieces completely, but it was probably good,
as then I was quite in control on the stage.
There were only 2 days after the headache went away
to prepare the Ghedini Concerto. It is also terribly difficult,
but I decided at the last moment to do it with the music.
It was broadcast all over Europe—with the Italian Radio
Orchestre of Turin, Mario Rossi conducted. Ghedini was a
great success.

One thing that made me very pleased in Vienna was that Joseph Krips, conductor of the San Francisco Symphony, and a Viennese, came to all 3 of my concerts and is just crazy about my playing. He is a great musician and a very nice man—I was always hoping to play for him. He asked me with whom I had studied, and then said, "But Kincaid never played like you—you are in your own world, no one ever comes near to you, etc." This means a lot to me, as you can understand, more than what critics write, although they were excellent, too. Krips called N.Y. at midnight after the Ibert and told a member of his board that he wants Efi and me in S. Francisco next season. He wants Ibert, but I think I would never live through it, unless I can change my psychological attitude to the piece in the meantime. I suffer too much. It is mostly torture.

The Viennese are steeped in Bach, Mozart and Beethoven but how they opened their hearts to Ibert and Ghedini! We always feel very much wanted in Vienna!

Prague Music Festival

"Once you cancel there is psychological permission to repeat the practice." This counsel came from her London physician when Elaine considered cancelling this tour to Czechoslovakia. The artist agreed with her doctor. There had been months of exhaustion after grueling hours of recording in London, and the strain of new works at the Vienna Festival. She had sought medical advice (*not feeling well since January*) and explored ways to eliminate the *little animals* in her system, namely amoeba. The treatment and tests would have decimated her energy and could have affected the heart.

Hotel Esplanade
Prague
31 May 1964

Dear Mother,
Last night was the concert. It was one of the greatest experiences of my career, and an audience I haven't seen anywhere. After Mozart, I came out for at least 10 minutes, 10-12 times. After Efi came out 10 times the whole audience rose, and screamed. He made a small speech and after that

102

came out several more times. We are the only Americans in the festival. The American Ambassador was there and sent us flowers.

We were offered concerts in Saltzburg next year and also 3 concerts in Turkey. Efi said I must have amoebas to play like I did last night. He thought it was one of the best Mozarts I have ever done.

Elaine returned to Switzerland to consult with the Cecil Clinic in Lausanne. It was ten years since her emergency appendectomy. *Am glad to say everything was excellent except that there are too few white cells, and now I am anemic! The doctor said I should avoid getting nervous—so I asked him how?*

The Edinburgh Festival

Scotland's famous Edinburgh Festival attracted international artists to the beautiful city where its imposing postcard castle overlooked the floral clock and manicured gardens that bordered Princes Street. Indeed, Elaine at last realized a long-held dream of playing in the prestigious annual festival held each August.

My husband and I were living in that charming city for two academic years while he earned his PhD degree. We had hoped Elaine would perform at the festival before the end of our stay.

Elaine came to visit us earlier, in 1954, for the special occasion of the baptism of our first son in St. Giles Cathedral. Her first nephew, she called the baby "Sir Gregory." Regretfully for us Elaine's performance was long after our two years abroad. Aaron had completed his graduate studies in theology and the three of us—my family—with "Sir Gregory" had returned to America.

Tantalizing comments by managers to Elaine in earlier years held out the plum status of The Edinburgh Festival. Elaine's recital took place on August 31, 1967 in Freemasons' Hall. This, her first concert after Kincaid's death, possibly accounted for it seeming *"more profound, as well as a new beginning."*

The following diligent critic's review spoke in entirety of what I had missed. Had I been there, my heart would have burst, my lips trembled, and my eyes moistened.

MARVELS OF FLUTE IN BACH SONATAS
C.M., *The Daily Telegraph,* Friday, September 1, 1967

Whatever other great performances this year's Edinburgh Festival has produced, or may yet produce, the one for which it will surely be best remembered, by those who heard it, is the recital by Elaine Shaffer and George Malcolm in the Freemasons' Hall today.

In four of Bach's Sonatas for flute and harpsichord, Miss Shaffer left no doubt that she is among the very greatest living musical artists. She proved that on this "orchestral" instrument, which composers from Mozart to Webern more or less ignored for solo purposes, it is possible to achieve as high a level of artistic expression and individuality as that so much more readily recognized in the art of say, Callas. Not one semiquaver, let alone any pair, slipped by as mere figuration without contributing to the rich melodic life and colour of the music; and so marvelously beautiful was the sound of the flute that sometimes a single note, such as her very first one in the third movement of the E minor Sonata, would have won back Eurydice.

And when a succession of such notes was spun into a long line, as in the first movement of the same sonata, or in either of the first two movements of the B minor, it would have been a strange listener, whose lips did not tremble, or whose eyes were not moist, at these divine strains.

George Hotel
Edinburgh
Sept. 2, 1967

Dear Mother,
Your letter came an hour before my concert. I really felt there were prayers holding me up, because my legs were shaking.

*The concert was sold-out for 3 weeks and a few minutes
before they said, "We are turning them away by the dozens."
One girl from Chicago said she waited in line for 4 hours to
get standing room.*

*Somehow the music had depth and communication—
you may remember when I saw a movie many years ago where
a violinist played and people cried and I said that is what I
want to be able to do. Efi said Mrs. Diamond cried (wife of
the festival manager), a fine pianist herself.*

*It was an ordeal, could have played better technically,
but many things were more profound than ever before.*

Elaine finished her performance and then attended her own choice of
a festival concert where Van Karajan conducted the Berlin Philharmonic.
A gentleman recognized her at intermission, "Miss Shaffer, for us, your
concert was the high point of the festival."

Geneva, 24 Oct. '65

Dear Daddie Rex & Mother
both for your letters
came

-4-

We visited Karl Barth in
hospital — he has been there
for 4 months with bladder trouble.
Seems it's really bad, and there's
not much that can be done for
him. He was so sorry to miss
the concerts, but I sent him
flowers and said we would
play for him. His younger son
was there the first night, and
his wife & daughter were there
second night — wonderful family,
and all so modest. He doesn't
look bad though, even though
he is so sick — he is concerned
about not being able to work —
imagine, at 80 yrs.! Am going
to ask Aaron & Bob to write him
a note. He said on the phone
before we left "Don't forget me
completely."
It was

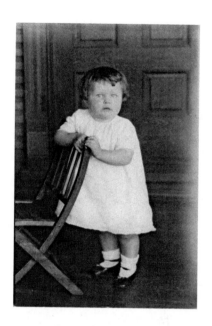

Elaine at age two

As a school girl

Elaine with William Kincaid and Maestro Ormandy

"For Elaine the Incomparable" Signed, Bill (Kincaid)

At the station in Gstaad

Village of Saanen in Switzerland

With Lily Pons in Montecatini   Keeping fit in St. Moritz

Swimming at Cap d'Antibes   At Palace Hotel in Gstaad

Bride and Groom with Bob Shaffer(left)

Le Pavillon home in Gstaad

Princess Margaret at Bath Festival

Queen Mother greets Elaine and Gerald Moore

Sir Jacob Epstein and Meissen Flute Player

Andres Segovia with Elaine and Efrem

Rehearsal with Yehudi Menuhin

Candlelight at Engadine Festival

With Hephzibah Menuhin and Efrem Kurtz

Recording studio with Yehudi Menuhin and son Jeremy

Mozart Flute and Harp Concerto with Zabaleto

Taking bows in Teatro San Carlo, Naples

Conducting debut in Lisbon

Israeli children with recorders

Recording Duo for Flute and Piano with Aaron Copland

Overlooking the Engadine Valley

September 2, 1967

Dear Mother,

We have spent the whole afternoon sending the reviews to lots of managers, etc. This morning I was antique-shopping with Mrs. Herbert von Karajan — she was a Paris model (about 35 yrs., maybe younger). Last night we were in the theatre and she came in, sat in the seat just next to ours. Her husband is here with his Berlin Philharmonic + she invited us to sit in her box tomorrow night. She seems to like me, for some reason, and I believe there has been a lot of talk about my concert, among all the festival artists. I didn't find anything to buy this morning — she collects little silver + enamel boxes. We saw a good production of Chekov's "The Cherry Orchard" last night.

Efi's back still bothers him, but I believe it's only the muscle.

Countries and Continents

The spiral of worldwide successes prompted Elaine to return to her own country and venture a New York debut. She needed the certainty of a warm reception expressed as: *I want to knock them dead in New York.* On a short six-week notice she appeared in recital in New York City's Town Hall on Friday, November 27, 1959.

Seventy hand-written invitations helped to make a reasonably full house and cover expenses. Efrem was not present as he had already agreed to prepare a series of all nine Beethoven Symphonies for the Canadian Broadcasting Symphony.

It's good that Robert (Weisz) and I play at least 3 recitals together before New York. There comes a point where the maximum is reached and the improvement comes from playing on the stage. This program of Mozart, Prokofieff, Schubert and Poulenc had been performed in London's Wigmore Hall six months earlier with ecstatic reviews.

> *New York Telegram and Sun,* Nov. 27, 1959
> **. . . consummate technic was only a medium for poetic communication. Always Miss Shaffer—like Mr. Weisz—was concerned with deeper truths and feelings, of which the beauty of sound was only the outer expression.**

> *New York Herald Tribune,* Nov. 28, 1959
> **Her homecoming was that of a mature, inspired and inspiring artist (whose) great gift is that of inherent musicality that will not let her play dully or meaninglessly. Here was music from three distinctly different periods, and Miss Shaffer was at home stylistically in each.**

Harold Schonberg, *New York Times,* Nov. 28, 1959
**Her playing was a little different from her male
counterparts. It was softer, more yielding, usually
more expressive, and with more rhythmic subtlety. She
held the audience's attention during her entire long
program and this in itself was a considerable feat.**

Beyond positive New York newspaper reviews, Sol Hurok's management,
in the person of the impresario himself, responded to Efrem that he now
must have Elaine under his name. Elaine quoted his verbiage "because
she is the greatest and I am the greatest." She welcomed this promising
development.

Israel

The Israel Philharmonic invited Efrem and Elaine for a twenty-one
day tour to perform in major areas in Israel. This trip had special appeal
to Elaine whenever she remembered her Sunday school's faded pictures of
those narrow, crowded streets and wandering shepherds. She appreciated
biblical history and read extensively of the development of the country
that had always fascinated her. Now she recalled references to Israel's place
within Christian prophecy.

Scheduled orchestra rehearsals and concerts demanded a large measure
of time. And there were Elaine's recitals between Tel Aviv, Haifa and
Jerusalem. Sightseeing during Shabbas, the Friday observance of Sabbath
relieved their heavy schedule. She walked the land of Palestine, the Holy
Land, and described it with pride and love. Elaine was living a youthful
dream.

Dan Hotel
Tel Aviv
28 January 1955

Dear Family,
*The people here love their country so much, and yet have
a certain air of sadness and oppression, combined with pride
in their history and accomplishments in building their own
state. They all love the ground they walk on and are verbally
optimistic about the future. When you think how they made
this state of Israel from nothingness, it is incredible. They all*

work very hard, but they have a sense of purpose: they know why they are working and what they are building. There are many sad faces, due to all of the beatings of the Nazis, etc. but you never see a bored face. Each individual has a history of suffering and wandering. They don't have money and the country is filled with problems, but I am sure that the majority are happier than the millionaires sitting on Miami Beach. If I were a Jew I would just want to stay here.

Today we went to see the incomplete shell of the new music hall which is being built (the orch. now repeats each program 10x because the old hall seats only 1100). The director of the Robin Hood Dell (Phila.), Freddie Mann gave them 250,000 dollars for the new hall. What a hall it will be! There will be 2800 seats.

Who will attend their concerts? Will it be a cold public as they were told, with an audience of only professors and scholars? Is it true that responses will be undemonstrative? Not so after the orchestra's warm reception, *even from the flute players.* At each performance ovations and curtain calls overwhelmed them. Playing in the beautiful city of Haifa, Elaine reported that, contrary to popular assessment, the Jewish audience proved their warm welcome and appreciation.

In Tel Aviv we had made a sensational hit. Everyone is raving and seems everyone knows us already. Dr. Salomin, mgr. of the orch., came to see me about doing a recital here and in Haifa, and he said that people stop him on the street and rave about us both. I want to do everything for them because they are all so nice. Besides this is invaluable experience and tremendous publicity.

Haifa
The hall was good and we played for 1800 people each night. They were completely mad about my playing (I did play well there). I came out five times, and they all came down to the front of the stage and cheered.

The owner of the Dan Hotel gave a reception at his home on Mt. Carmel, overlooking Haifa Bay. Everyone acted as if I

*were a queen and Efrem a king. They said the most flattering
things, and they don't say it if they <u>don't</u> mean it.*

Jerusalem Post, February 6, 1955
**Elaine Shaffer's performance of the Mozart Concerto
was impeccable.**

Zmanim, February 11, 1955
**Miss Elaine Shaffer, the first flautist to come here,
succeeded in lifting the Jerusalem audience out of its
usual coolness, and brought it to a justified excess of
enthusiasm by the polish and perfection of her playing
and her truly beautiful musical taste.**

Their reception and success matched that of former soloists Marian
Anderson, Artur Rubinstein and Jascha Heifetz. An Associated Press
reporter addressed her: "Jerusalem has been conquered 57 times by many
armies. But tonight you have conquered it for the 58th time. They come
with many dresses and with each change they perform worse and worse—
you have only 2 dresses and each performance is better and better."

Concerts were sold out; some who had tickets to one concert requested
more. One respected pianist told Efrem that Elaine had one of the greatest
successes since the founding of the Philharmonic. Invitations to socialize
made demands they could not always honor.

*We had to refuse the Prime Minister in Jerusalem and
the U.S. Ambassador and his wife. It really wears you out,
talking to Jews, or should I say <u>listening</u>, but they are so nice.
And I never saw so much food.*

Efrem penned in his oversize print:

ELAINE WAS A SENSATION. I WILL NEVER
UNDERSTAND HOW SHE DID IT—NOW THIS ANGEL
UNDERSTANDS WHY CHRIST WENT ON THE
MOUNTAIN (TO REST)—THE JEWS DON'T LET YOU
ALONE. YOU MUST EAT! YOU MUST TELL EVERYTHING!
YOU MUST NOT SLEEP! YOU MUST BE WITH US—
NEVER MIND TO BE ALONE! WHAT A NATION!
GREETINGS TO YOU ALL, (signed) ONE OF THEM

A hotel by the sea would seem ideal for chronic asthma, sneezing and allergies, but each day Elaine ordered a massage for relief.

Tel Aviv
11 February 1955
They have taken everything but blood here, and I am feeling
it. In Haifa it took five cups of coffee to have energy to get on
stage. Then I shook so noticeably I could hardly take bows.

Sabbath in the city of Jerusalem:

The whole city from Mt. Zion is a most impressive sight,
impossible to describe. We saw King David's tomb, orthodox
Jews praying, facing the old city (impassable now because it
is in Arab hands). They pray that they can go back because it
is the holy part. The new city for them is sinful.
Later we went to a section where only orthodox Jews
live. It was really interesting to see the beards, the long curls
where side-burns should be. Their markets have a special
smell and nothing is very clean, but today they were scrubbing
in preparation for the Sabbath. The other Jews do not like
the Orthodox ones, because they are anti-Zionist, against
the state of Israel, and they don't like the more liberal ones
to be allowed to come in. It is the same in all religions; the
fanatics don't do anyone any good and they spend their time
criticizing. It is a striking sight to see the old orthodox ones,
who hold to the keeping of the law, etc. the same as in the
Old Testament days.

The Hebrew Newspaper in Tel Aviv interviewed Elaine to learn about her views on Zionism. Her statement incorporated her long-held beliefs.

Dear Beverly,
I am grateful for this opportunity, as a kind of missionary
work, even greater than a missionary would have, because
of already being established in the country as a name, even
in a relatively short time. All of this is an experience I shall
never forget. It is strange, but I always have the feeling that I
will be coming back here, because it has been a unique time
in my life.

129

Reading these words, I knew the internal struggle Elaine waged as a schoolgirl. Was her life-calling to be a missionary rather than a musician? This invitation to perform in Israel, the accolades, ovations and hospitality, gratified her as an artist, with even further satisfaction as she entered the everyday world of Israeli citizens.

Three opportunities touched Elaine's ambition to share her gifts with these people. First, the Israel Philharmonic invited her to play at their monthly performance for the Army Military Reserve, a service required once a month for orchestra members under 49 years of age.

> *They all whistled just like the American boys when I came out, and I thought they were not going to be quiet. In the intermission, the commanding officer said that he wished he knew the secret of keeping them so quiet for such a long time! We were both presented with speeches and gold pins of the regiment.*

The children at a Kibbutz school also responded to the Americans. Efrem spoke to them in English (not the usual custom) and told them stories of Elaine and her flute.

> *They came back stage for autographs. They were wonderful, so beautiful too. They behave so well and are terribly serious and quietly self-confident. The people are so proud of their children, as they are the future of Israel. They were really inspiring to see when I went to visit the school. They presented me with a recorder, and I am having great fun playing it. They call it a flute in Hebrew. A.P. made a story with pictures.*

During one of the many receptions, Elaine innocently promoted the long overdue need for a concert hall in Tel Aviv. Dr. Hale, the head of America's Point-Four Program, was also a guest.

> *I had just seen the new hall being built (the new Mann auditorium) in Tel Aviv and said (to Dr. Hale) how much it is needed. Surprisingly enough, a day later the manager of the orchestra told me that Dr. Hale had been invited for that*

very purpose; they are hoping to get money from the Point-Four program. The management could not very well beg, so I did a more effective job, without even knowing it! Later, Dr. H. came to the concert and was very excited. Afterward, the manager came to me and almost kissed me and said they are quite sure that they will get the money, and that it is only because I spoke to Dr. Hale about the hall! He brought another American from the Point-Four to the concert, a Dr. Foy, who is a good friend of Dr. Nancarrow [our high school principal]!

Elaine's long impassioned letters continued to span the distance that isolated her family when she yearned to share this privileged world with them.

Author Scholem Asch came to another concert. I spoke with him for quite a while. He thinks that my flute sounds like it is praying when he listens. He told me a beautiful story about an ignorant shepherd boy who did not know the Hebrew prayers, but every time he wanted to pray, he would lie down on the ground and whistle. One day on a high holiday he went into the synagogue, where everyone was praying. Since he didn't know the prayers he began to whistle. Then the rabbi heard him and suddenly realized that this was prayer too, then made a sermon about it.

Asch is expressive as a man. He has a face much like Albert Schweitzer. The Jews do not like the way he writes. He is too much inclined to Christianity for them, especially the Orthodox. He gave me a Hebrew book, The Nazarene, with his autograph, and wrote in my book, With Admiration. He and his wife plan to come to my concerts in London.

Another impressive man whom Elaine came to know, Dr. Spiro, was not a recognized name, but to Elaine, *one of the greatest men I have ever met.*

This outstanding orthopedic surgeon came to the concerts and to dinner. He could have made millions in private practice, but he chose to be in the Israel Army, and to serve only the soldiers. He gets about 150 dollars a month, and works terribly long hours, but he would rather be in this country than any other. Dr. Spiro told us that when he first started to work during the Arab war, he went to the hardware store and bought his operating tools! Then someone told us that he went during the fighting, dodging bombs on the street to look for silk to make stitches. He is a humble man. There are many stories of how he has helped people without accepting a fee, and even paying from his own pocket.

Eighteen performances in as many days was a once-in-a-lifetime experience, a wonderful opportunity to play so many times.

The concerts halls are so small that repeats of the same program are necessary. I played to 30,000 different people. Amazing in such a small country. Now I am not as nervous and feel much more at home with the audience.

February 12, 1955
Interest from the concert managers in a return engagement will require negotiations if there is to be a contract. We will not come back until the new hall is built and then it will not be necessary to do so many concerts. The extensive publicity and their generous gifts compensated for a less than adequate fee.

I will cry, I know, before the last regular concert.

No one can really know about Israel unless he has seen it. There is something about this country which you cannot explain with words.

Twelve years later Elaine returned to Israel, as she believed she would. Did she hope to revive the emotional impact of her initial visit when all her senses had been enlivened? Could so many changes have taken place? Whatever the untenable professional environment, the visit concluded early.

Geneva
3 March 1967
We left Israel early because I played only 2½ concerts— cancelled 5. Orchestra terrible—conductor impossible and rude to me besides—artistic director insulting. I offered to go on with a different conductor, or to conduct myself, but

they had to protect their <u>local boy</u>, a kibbutz man who picks apples as a job, and has hardly ever conducted a concert. It was aggravating and nerve wracking as I really had to <u>fight</u>. The result was an attack of asthma—had to call a doctor at 4 AM. Now it has all developed into bronchitis and bad sinusitis.

Australia

Australia was a long, lonely trip of forty hours by air, even on Britannia, the new BOAC plane Whispering Giant. Elaine had little hope that she would perform at all. She packed one concert dress, just in case schedules got jinxed, and chose a limited winter wardrobe. Efrem had already settled in Adelaide and had begun rehearsals for the six-week engagement with the Australian Broadcast Concerts. Elaine hoped to lighten his spirits as he prepared to conduct in major cities and smaller towns on this vast continent.

(probably Adelaide)
11 July 1957

Dear Mother,

We feel as if we are in prison. I am waiting for Aug. 15th to go away to Switzerland. We are almost starved, because the food is lousy. We have been invited to homes that were absolutely freezing and the people are frozen too. There are the silly newspaper interviews and now a woman reporter phoned to find out what I am going to wear tonight to the concert. The hall is not heated at all, so I would like to go wrapped in a blanket, like an Indian. I've only got one dress and they wrote about that the other day. She can say "the same old dress." Efi is performing and they write about me.

Lennons Hotel
Brisbane
18 July 1957

Dear Mother,

Efi went to a Dr. yesterday as he felt tired, but there is nothing wrong, only too much Australia. His first concert is tomorrow and then we are off to Melbourne <u>where I am playing</u>. There is another silly reception this afternoon.

Menzies Hotel
Melbourne
24 July 1957

Dearest Daddie Rex and Mother,

We are both in bed with Asian Flu, sore throats and fever. There is a terrible epidemic. Efi has cancelled 2 concerts, but we are supposed to play on Saturday night together and I don't know if I will be strong enough to blow. They want me to play (with another conductor). I still have a temperature, even with the strong medicine, a new discovery, mycin (?) drug.

The doctor is advising Efi to cancel because they are afraid he will not be all right for the 9 concerts in Sydney.

(Later that day) Now they have cancelled the Sat. concert, so I am not playing. Your letter means so much, being on this planet. Efrem in one of his own inimitable statements, said, "the people here only live to exist!!" Perhaps it would sound better in Russian.

27 July 1957

Dearest Bev,

This whole country reminds us of Texas—someone said it is like USA was 50 years ago. There is something depressing about being so far away from the rest of the world. One thing it has done for us, we appreciate much more, many little things in Europe we took almost for granted. Many Europeans migrated and they can earn more money but they miss the culture; none here to speak of.

The orchestras are terrible except for Melbourne and Sydney and even in these they have no style, just play notes. Besides, the musicians are arrogant and talk back to conductors because there is a shortage of players. The strong union will not allow more than 10% foreigners in orchestras.

They certainly squeeze everything out of the artists on these tours. The poor girl, Leontyne Price (negro singer from USA), has been here eleven weeks and she is almost dead. She said, "Let's face it—Ah've had it!"

The Australia Hotel
Sydney
8 August 1957

Dear Daddie Rex and Mother,

I want you to know of the excitement here! At the rehearsal for the opening subscription concert the piano soloist, Bussotti, was playing and in the middle of it he said he couldn't go on. (Efrem had predicted that he couldn't play and told me to bring the music and my flute to rehearsal.) The ABC executives were in a huddle and in three minutes asked me to take his place. The concert was that night! I felt like a football player warming up on the side lines, while Efi rehearsed.

I played also Thursday and Saturday. Monday and tonight another concerto. The audience made a huge ovation knowing I was a last minute substitution. Besides, I am playing at the launching of the OPERA FUND DRIVE, a great honor and soloists will have their names engraved in the new opera house on a plaque. They asked me to play again on Sunday for the Popular Concert.

I got a terrific fee agreement, double what I was to be paid in Melbourne for the one concert that was cancelled.

Have not felt well, played the 2nd night with a blinding headache.

Nothing could be done about Efrem's final concert in Perth. They must each travel alone to leave behind what they termed The Planet.

Efi was still scheming as I left, to be excused from his last 2 concerts. It is a shame, because he worked so hard and had great success in Sydney, where the orchestra is first-class, and now to Perth where they couldn't play if Toscanini conducted.

Now the ABC is surprised and kicking themselves that they didn't engage me for the whole tour which is exactly what I wanted to make them feel! We not only had ovations at the concerts but our friends say that the whole town is talking about us.

> *I was on the radio "Women's Session" and they thought*
> *I would talk about clothes because they loved all my "frocks"*
> *(all 2 of them).*

Expressive excerpts from two Sydney press reviews were worth carrying away.

The Sun, August 1957
Flautist Star of Concert—fascinating performance—
air of deep concentration.

Canon, September 1957
In Elaine Shaffer we met not only a charming
personality, but an artist of deep musical insight
and feeling. The playing of Mozart's K 313 and 314
was interpretive and of the highest possible quality,
profoundly inspiring.

Final conversations with the management about the success of the tour hinted of a return engagement in two years. To themselves, Elaine and Efrem muttered their favorite expression, "We have been to Australia *twice*—the first and last time!" That would be their final sentiment.

Japan

Elaine, as a young schoolgirl, carried an image of Japan, a frightening distant country at war with her own homeland. As a performing artist, she and her husband accepted an invitation to take their music to this unfamiliar land in 1962. NHK Radio hosted their two-month tour playing orchestral works and solos. Elaine and Efrem were intrigued by the curious language, culture, and people.

> *Imperial Hotel*
> *Tokyo*
> *11 April 1962*

Dear Daddie Rex,
> *Our long trip with no sleep in 36 hours, took us to Hong*
> *Kong—a great experience, one of the most beautiful places*
> *we have ever seen. Chinese people are so wonderful and still*

serve with dignity and kindness. Now I understand why
the missionaries always loved China. A 3½ hour flight to
Tokyo landed us at 9.00 PM, met by floodlights, many press
photographers, then an interview where we were presented
with ten bouquets. Next morning a meeting with president
of NHK Radio, and a press conference with about thirty-five
reporters to learn details of the Tokyo tour.

The Imperial is an old hotel designed by Frank Lloyd
Wright. Our 2ⁿᵈ floor suite is cozy and they promptly provide
any amenity. We asked NHK for a radio and TV, and within
a half hour they arrived, both brand new!

In the small rehearsal room of a special building used by
the orchestra, I can practice mornings and afternoons and
also write letters. NHK gave me a typewriter in this room—
paper, stamps, everything. We eat our own sandwiches here.
There is tea when we arrive in the morning, at intermissions,
and at end of rehearsals, a total of 5 times a day.

There is no tipping, a pleasure. We wanted to give money
to the girl who brought our tea—she wouldn't take it, so I
bought her a blouse, and she was so happy.

An early impression of the busy city streets reminded them of New York
City, except for lower buildings and crowds somehow not as suffocating.
Amazingly, in the midst of the masses of people, the public seemed to
maintain their perfect manners. Some said their finest manners are most
on display in the home.

Elaine practiced about twenty Japanese words that she had learned for
greetings and conversation.

> *Tokyo*
> *17 April 1962*

Dear Mother,
Many problems are due to the language, such as when
they brought our breakfast at 10.30 at night! We had ordered
it for 8 the next morning. One comes every day at 11.30 and
asks: Do you hope lunch today? Already we are talking to
them the way they talk.

11 May 1962

Dearest Beverly,
    Your letter arrived in an accumulated stack. They apologized, but there were some near disasters because of some of the delayed letters. The hotel is paying for any cable we had to send because of their neglect.
    There is complete silence during whole rehearsals—no one talks. Amazing discipline of audience, no talking at all, no coughing or moving around, but applauding a lot. People in the audience bring presents. One young boy brought me a lion's head carved in wood, supposed to bring good luck.
    Efi has passed the difficult days and now everything goes smoothly. He is incredible though, how he keeps optimistic in the midst of real trial—any other conductor would just give up trying to communicate with those stone faces. But you should see them all now—everyone smiles, they are completely free, and the music is quite different, very warm and even emotional sometimes. I believe they were waiting to see whether or not they were accepted, not deciding whether or not they liked Efi. Japanese have a tremendous need to be accepted, to bring honor to their family, ancestors, etc. The worst thing anyone could do is sneer at them. Still it is a mysterious country and people in many ways, and I'm sure one could never feel that they understood it completely. The moment you think you have something figured out, you see it is not the answer at all. We saw a film, Bridge to the Sun, a rather drippy movie, a true story, about Japanese customs.
    I played for the first time—the Mozart Flute and Harp Concerto with Zabeleta. The audience was engaged and I thought they would never stop applauding. So many saw us on TV and afterward we were recognized in shops and in the hotel. I have four more solo appearances, the Mozart G major Concerto (subscription concert) and the Bach Suite No. 2.

(There were no translations of several news clippings of the concerts and the western guests' appearances.)
    A car and chauffeur at their disposal was convenient for short trips to shop for necessities. The driver spoke a little English. The shops displayed some amazing Japanese technology in wonders such as a Sony five-inch

television and transistor radio the size of a cigarette box. Elaine described it in several letters and, even though it would only work within the country, she made the purchase, possibly thinking of the launching of the space shuttle, since the astronaut Yuri Gagarin was staying at their hotel.

> *Today I bought myself a present; a Japanese fishing rod—it is beautiful, folds up into a little case, good for bait and flies.*

Hours in The Silk Gallery were spent selecting fabulous fabrics as gifts for mother or me. She bought scarves and a kimono dressing gown for herself. The other precious commodity was cultured pearls. At the Mikimoto shop she honored her family's selections. We chose pearl necklaces, earrings, or brooches.

In the midst of the unbelievably crowded Tokyo streets a tourist from Houston recognized Efrem. She was Mrs. Sakowitz, mother of the owner of the Texas department store. Elaine and Efrem were too tired to consider their invitation to join them for some Tokyo night life.

> *May 2, 1962*
>
> Dear Mother,
>
> *I am dreaming of the salads in Switzerland. I have salmon every day (and Efi his steaks). The strawberries are good. They are huge and we wash them in hot water.*
>
> *We have tried several restaurants, German, Russian, etc., but none are as good as the hotel.*
>
> *Walt Sheldon, from Philadelphia, who used to announce Curtis broadcasts, now production manager of Armed Forces Far East Network (U.S.A.) and his Japanese wife Yuki, took us to a Japanese inn, sitting on the floor before a low table. Two waitresses, sitting there to serve and fill one's sake cup—a variety of items, all artistically arranged.*
>
> *In the middle of playing in the big hall for TV, my asthma came on—maybe from the raw fish (?). I was awake all night.*
>
> *The U. S. Ambassador's office (Reischauer) phoned saying he will not be at our concert, but we will be invited to his residence. They say he writes Japanese better than Japanese*

scholars, and of course speaks perfectly—(married to a Japanese woman).

The driver was to take us to Nikko (possibly the National Park) but Efi had an infected tooth. On Sunday we took advantage of the opportunity to greet the Emperor on his birthday at the Imperial Palace grounds. Over 90,000 people went during the day and it was interesting to see how well-behaved the crowds were—no one pushed or shouted.

Also have been to Hakone to view Mt. Fuji. It was a pleasure to be outside of Tokyo where the city is so dirty, nothing stays clean. It is as bad as Altoona or Liverpool.

Went to a Zen Buddhist temple, a place of peace set in a beautiful garden. The gardens are places to go for quiet if you have the energy and determination to get there. Of course this week was a National Holiday.

Tokyo
April 24, 1962

Dear Beverly,

Went to the Tokyo Union Church for Good Friday and on Easter afternoon. More than half the congregation was Japanese. Will go to the Synagogue for Passover with Efi. (I want to see what a Japanese Jew looks like!)

The tour is nearly complete and orchestra members say the NHK Symphony never had so much success in its history. After the three consecutive subscription concerts the orchestra sent me flowers.

I am leaving in 10 minutes—about 30 people coming to airport from NHK, so I cannot cry! Must remember the Japanese custom of never showing one's feeling in public.

Because of her schedule with the Bath Festival in England, Elaine returned to Europe alone. On each of five stopovers, (Manila, Bangkok, Karachi, Teheran, and Rome), she missed Efrem's company. Earthquake rumblings felt in Japan made him more reluctant than usual to finish the tour without her.

Japan Revisited

Elaine and Efrem registered at The Imperial Hotel again in January 1967, five years after their first tour. On this trip via Hawaii, Elaine located the house in Honolulu where William Kincaid had lived. The photographs were mementos to share with "Bill" on a future trip to Philadelphia.

> *Imperial Hotel*
> *Tokyo*
> *16 January 1967*

Dear Daddie Rex and Mother,

My ability to adjust has not improved. It's grey and smoggy, my eyes burn and nose runs. I suppose we will see things differently when we are more rested. We are 14 hours ahead of your time. Efi's first concert is tomorrow—he is pleased with the orchestra—likes it better than the one he had in 1962. There are two boys from the Boston Symphony in it. The first violin is also from America—used to be with Toscanini.

Dr. Eitel [whom Elaine knew from 1962] *took me to see the new Olympic stadium—it certainly is magnificent and will probably be standing many years from now. He also gave me some drops for low blood pressure which have helped to make me feel more alive. He is such a wonderful man.*

> *Imperial Hotel*
> *Tokyo*
> *23 January 1967*

Dear Beverly,

Have been particularly disturbed because of the concert coming up and didn't feel like working at all. I felt really low and couldn't get out of it. Yesterday we went to the steam bath and had a marvelous massage, and I feel <u>much</u> better. Went again today. My concert is almost sold out and has been for two months. They say if all the flute players in Tokyo came it would fill the hall. Then we go to Kyoto for five days.

We met a wonderful couple, Jerry Schechter and wife, bureau chief of <u>Time-Life</u>—(both 34 years old)—he interviewed me about the new concerto I'm playing, but

Time didn't want to do the story this week—maybe next week. I don't believe it, from past experience. He just finished a book on Buddhism—very sensitive boy. He did a cover story on Japan for Time.

We were at their home for dinner—they have 5 children under 12. She was talking about their life, how they met when they were 17, and she waited for him "to grow up." Then she saw him becoming a professional man and she had to take each step up with him. They are rare people. His wife's mother lives with them and she cooks the most fabulous Russian Jewish things. It was really great!

Reviews covered two premieres on the second concert.

Marcel Grilli, *The Japan Times*, February 1, 1967
Elaine Shaffer brought to Japan Ernest Bloch's Two Last Poems (maybe?) and Funeral Music and Life Again for Flute and Orchestra written for E.S. (January 1958). Each poem a subtle interplay of phrases tinged with somberness and sadness. Miss Shaffer played this music with deep feeling and affection. Following this first performance in Japan, Miss Shaffer introduced a Flute Concerto in D Minor, by Franz Danzi which she herself had only recently discovered . . . in the musty archives of a German library . . .

7 February 1967

Dear Daddie Rex,

Our last day in Japan. Efi's concert on Sunday was crowded with people standing. (The management had expected their usual 60% of capacity.) They already wrote Hurok asking for Efi to come back for a longer period, also for me to play "many" times.

Yesterday we were at lunch at the Italian Embassy and had the Swiss Ambassador as our guest last night at dinner. Lunch today with Jerry Schechter of Time *magazine—a great guy!*

Tonight is the last concert. The orchestra is giving us a party after the concert.

*Toshiba Co. (who produces our records here) gave me a
beautiful AM-FM radio—I chose it from their show room.
I will write more from Israel.*

Love to you and Mother,
Elaine

Russia

"You must go to Russia. You will be a sensation!" Sol Hurok assured
Elaine of future concerts under his management. She confided, *I told him*
[Russia] *was my only ambition.*

*Funny, going to USSR feels like going to the moon. It
is not so far, but seems further than Japan or Australia—
there are other ways of measuring distance besides miles or
kilometers.*

Elaine practiced overtime—eight and nine hours a day—once the
reality of a tour in Russia sank in. She wanted to perform at her very
best, as she imagined a Russian would do when appearing in the West.
Also, this tour validated Sol Hurok's management and confidence in
her success.

For Efrem the invitation meant a return to his native country, a
trip he thought unimaginable many years ago. He left Russia with his
family and many others of Jewish heritage in 1917 during the Bolshevik
Revolution. At that time the city known as St. Petersburg became
Leningrad.

Three Russian cities, Moscow, Leningrad, and Kiev, honored Elaine
and Efrem's performances. Efrem conducted local orchestras in each city.
Elaine performed four major works by Bach, Mozart, and Bloch.

Leningrad A direct flight to Leningrad was impossible in 1966. They
landed instead in Moscow where they were met by Nina, an interpreter,
who assisted Elaine with language and customs while Efrem felt at home
using his native tongue. A comfortable night train to Leningrad had clean
beds in large compartments and tea available anytime. Long lines of men
waiting to shave formed in front of one room, the first of many lines, a way
of life in each city they visited.

Hotel Metropole
April 24, 1966

As we went from the station to the hotel Efi remembered the name of every street, all important buildings and monuments. The view from our hotel room was of the concert hall where a block-long line of people waited, hoping to get a returned ticket because they had been sold out for two weeks. The hotel was clean and the old maid was pleased that Efi had not forgotten his Russian!

Leningrad's historic beauty remained, clearly a highlight of the tour. Picturesque canals resembled Venice or Amsterdam. However, a close up view of the ravages of war and the reality of food shortages and inadequate housing reminded them of Russia's sad history.

An emotional family reunion on the train platform faded forty-seven bygone years. "Your aunt is there to meet you—the one in the middle with the flowers," Nina announced. There stood Lyda, Efi's aunt, seventy-eight years old, his mother's youngest sister, with daughters born after Efi left. He distracted himself from the tearful moment to acknowledge the orchestra members on hand.

Sumptuous hospitality overwhelmed them with each poignant family visit.

We went to dinner at the relatives. I wanted to take a Danish Cheese as a gift. Well, you should have seen the table. So much food I haven't seen in ages, all home-made Russian things. After trying everything for an hour, we thought that was all, but then came meat, veal chops beautifully cooked with carrots and potatoes. Then two huge chocolate cakes. It was probably a week's salary spent. There was so much fun and laughter and a festive spirit. I couldn't bear to give them the cheese after that!

(Food shops offered good black bread, yogurt, buttermilk and a few apples. Caviar is plentiful. Everything is terribly expensive for them, except rents.)

Before their first rehearsal with the Leningrad Philharmonic, the couple took advantage of a performance with its regular conductor, Mravinsky. The orchestra held a wide reputation as one of the greatest.

> *The hall is a gem, white columns, red seats, and magnificent chandeliers on the ceilings. We found the audience cool, and the orchestra was still and formal, no one smiling. Efi said "when I get them they will smile."*
>
> *At the second rehearsal the orchestra is tremendously enthusiastic about both of us. The flutists all want sources for music and records.*
>
> *The people jammed into the hall for the first concert, many standing. We somehow felt that every concert ever given before this one was only a preparation; this one really mattered! The audience applauded with tremendous enthusiasm, everyone smiling, including the orchestra. Efi conducted Beethoven Fifth like someone possessed, with incredible power. The orchestra responded with all they had. Here special warmth was added, as if they were welcoming one of their own, returning to his "home town."*
>
> *The audience response after the second concert was even more enthusiastic. After my Mozart, the two cousins, Zinna and Asia, brought little bouquets to me on the stage. The audience applauded in unison for a long time, even after the Bach Suite, Mozart Concerto and an encore. I could have played a few more encores in each concert, but wanted to leave them fresh for Efi's Beethoven Fifth.*

Beyond music making they relished rare opportunities to connect with family, to take meals with them, and to look about the homestead recalled from Efi's youth.

> *The front door of the house is the same but everything terribly run down; almost what would be considered a slum in America. Inside the house he left 47 years ago the kitchen appears exactly the same, except that now 8 families use it. As if from nowhere, an abundance of incredible food is spread for "tea." Two photographs of his grandmother and grandfather hang on the wall. A bed, table, chairs, TV, and refrigerator leave hardly room to move. Outside is a beautiful bridge for foot traffic, with 2 lions on each end. The canal*

runs by the house. It must have been beautiful, and it would be today with a little paint and fixing up.

Leningrad meant a tour of the wondrous Hermitage Museum with its famous French Impressionist collection. Its enormity made it impossible to survey it all.

The Russian Easter coincided that year with its Western observance. Elaine hoped to attend the pageantry of the midnight mass but news of the incredible crowds deterred her. Rehearsal schedules interfered with her Easter Sunday attendance in the Baptist church.

The final Leningrad Philharmonic concert included a tribute from the concertmaster to both musicians. A profound and sincere reply from Efi made clear that the time together had been all too short.

Moscow After the wonderful experiences of Leningrad frustrating incidents loomed. The Party Congress occupied the best hotel, the National. Accommodations offered them in exchange were hardly deluxe. Instead, the gloomy, impossible room and bathroom must do. Compared to Leningrad, Moscow was ugly. Many more people, big city traffic and hundreds of blocks of dreary apartment houses created a depressing atmosphere.

The American Ambassador Kohler welcomed them to the Embassy on the first morning and thanked them for coming at such a time when relations between the countries were low, saying, "We need you badly." When they asked "Is there something we could do for our country?" the Ambassador replied, "Just have a success and you will have made your contribution." The Ambassador's news conference mentioned the concert and alerted the press to attend.

The orchestra was good, but not as good as Leningrad's. The Conservatory served as the concert hall, a big beautiful hall, with excellent acoustics. Around the walls were portraits of composers.

From my position on the stage, Mozart and Bach were looking down at me, side by side. (The son of Shostakovich, who is a conductor, was at all the rehearsals.) The evening concert was very exciting. I played just as I wanted to, and was controlled and calm. The audience went wild. The orchestra itself made half of the ovation and the audience was impressed by that. All the important musicians, critics, professors, etc. were in the audience as well as all the international *wire services. Afterward the <u>N.Y. Times</u> Bureau Chief, Peter Grose, had a party for us at his apartment. The most important Moscow musicologist and critic was there and he was ecstatic about our concert. He has been often in other countries, has heard other flutists, and said he never heard anything like my way of playing. He said it was a historical event for Russia, because they never had a foreign flutist and they didn't know a flute could do those things. Jacqueline du Pré was there, the English girl cellist, who is studying for 6 months with Rostropovich. She has been going to concerts for 2 months in Moscow and said she never saw such excitement in the hall as for us.*

Ambassador Kohler and his wife attended the final concert and afterward hosted dinner at the ambassador's residence. Impeccable Chinese waiters served a marvelous meal. The only other guests were Mr. Weiner, Counselor for Cultural Affairs, with his wife, and Peter Groce of the *New York Times.* In this comfortable, secure atmosphere, they exchanged tales of frustration dealing with Russian hotel service, mail deliveries, orchestra members' arrogance, etc.

The Ambassador's formula when dealing with Russians is: Be Firm, Persistent, Patient, and Polite. Mr. Kohler had a funny story about throwing his old suit in a waste basket, as they are not allowed to give things to their Russian servants. Four months later it came to him by <u>post</u> in America!

Kiev Humor in helpless situations in Russia relieved tensions, especially with air travel. Planes may make funny noises, Elaine relayed, but not to worry: *The pilots catch the devil when they don't bring the planes back!* For this trip each carried his own luggage, waited for a ladder to board the plane and, with more delay, stood freezing in the cold wind. Efrem was habitually nervous about plane trips and with the strange noises he easily believed this flight would be his last.

The hour flight delivered them into a warm Riviera-like climate with flowers and green grass, beautiful parks, and the Dnieper River in the background. They were met by the son-in-law of Khrushchev, an obscure figure, once having been director of the Opera House. Now, director of the symphony, he relayed surprising news such as one concert instead of two, the date moved up one day, and thereby hardly enough time for proper rehearsals with a third-rate orchestra. All of these idiosyncrasies were part of the mysteries of this trip.

In Kiev a flute player tried an annoying distraction back stage before her solo performance. Insolence from one of the horn players annoyed Efi enough to "put him in his place."

Before I came on the stage the flutist was playing my Mozart Concerto, a lot of other pieces, all very loud and fast, without stopping. He had studied in Paris, and therefore felt superior to everyone around him. Anyway, after I finished playing, the whole orchestra applauded for 5 minutes, and he came to me absolutely broken. He couldn't find words for his admiration, etc. My suspicions were confirmed by some of the other orchestra people, of whom 80% are Jews, that the flutist is the worst anti-Semite of any. We later heard that Kiev is the worst anti-Semitic center in Russia, and the Israel Orchestra will not play there. The Jewish players were adorable; they stayed after rehearsals to listen to Efi talk, and wanted us to stay with them to tell about our life. The other flutists came with millimeter measuring devices to measure the holes in my flute, so they could cut holes like it in theirs—(to sound the same, perhaps??).

Attendance at the evening concert was attended by members of the Iowa University Symphonic Band, a State Dept. sponsored tour. The band included 11 girl flutists in the front row. The ovation was tremendous after my part, and they all stood up and presented flowers, while photos were taken. AP wrote a story "Iowa meets Pennsylvania in Kiev."

During the second half, while the audience was applauding like mad, in unison, Efi was backstage screaming to get that second horn out of his sight. (He had played deliberately louder than necessary and wrong notes, just being nasty.) The boy came at intermission and asked, "What did I do?" Efi said, "If you don't know what you did, then go home and think about it. I never want to see you again." So the symphony was done with a horn missing, though one hardly noticed it. One of the Jewish members with a particularly beautiful facial expression, full of stories that could not be told, came to Efi and said, "We are thankful to you for doing what we cannot do."

Before the flight back to Moscow, they made personal phone calls to violinist Gilels and composer Khachaturian. The composer was in bed with a broken leg.

He [Khachaturian] has made the first sketch of my flute concerto and will send it. Shostakovich's son told his father that I am the Rostropovich of the flute and he must write a concerto. He is now busy on an opera.

The big boss from Gosconcert came to say good bye, and asked us to forget the unpleasant things that were beyond their control and asked us back in the 1967-68 season. The tour had been a triumph.

Elaine's diary of each experience that warmed her heart or aroused her curiosity during the two-week stay became eleven pages, typed single-space, certainly not trusted to the mails until after she had left the country.

The strongest impressions are still the marvelous spirit of the people, their enthusiasm, love of life, and their insatiable curiosity about the outside world. I am convinced that there should be more free exchange of people from both sides, because just as they have been indoctrinated with the unfavorable aspects of our society, we have been shown and brought up to believe a somewhat colored version of theirs.

One comes to see the unimportance of the creature comforts we feel to be necessary, and the tremendous amount of printed matter we have access to and take for granted. It makes one feel like not wasting a moment in learning, when one sees their tremendous drive for studying and knowing, and not being allowed to read what they would like to, or go where they may wish to go. There is so much to be learned from these people's attitude to life.

South Africa

An invitation to visit the City of Johannesburg on this exotic continent promised breathtaking beauty and eye-opening culture for Elaine. Efrem was engaged to conduct the National Symphony Orchestra of the SABC in a series of concerts in October 1971. Elaine's performance of two solos prompted her to request an "extra" appearance which brought its own personal satisfaction.

Elaine made the long flight of nearly twenty-four hours with some misgivings. Once more, her own schedule precluded travelling with her husband and, before leaving Switzerland, she began to acknowledge mysterious symptoms of discomfort that more than one doctor tried to ease. She agreed to a series of medications for relief of neck pain. *It's a disk problem due to over-use in my profession. I am only comfortable when I lie flat.*

Nausea and headache confounded the speedy drive from Gstaad to the Geneva airport, possibly the affect of the prescribed medicine. Mid-flight, while using the bathroom, she accidentally caught her finger in the metal refuse door. The ragged, deep cut flowed with blood.

> *I told the steward and he said as soon as he finished serving he would look at it. I said "You must do something now." He offered me a Band Aid from his firstaid box. I began to worry about tetanus, so I asked for vodka, and soaked the finger for about 2 hours in the best Polish vodka! By that time the headache was gone and I got cramps in the stomach.*

Soon after arriving in this magnificent city, Elaine sensed the appalling political situation, a world of extreme contrasts: beauty and luxury against isolation and deprivation. Apartheid existed, allowing very real injustice for a segment of South African citizens in outlying isolated townships. Concerts held in Johannesburg's City Hall prevailed for whites only.

> *We play for the regular concert series on Oct. 26 and 27. Then on the 28th for the Bantu people (blacks) in their township Boi Ketlong. This is a rare thing; no one has done it for at least 15 years and never an American. We asked to do it and will not take a fee. I am looking forward to that.*

At this event, Efrem first conducted Beethoven, and then Elaine followed with her own Mozart *Concerto*. A glimpse of the 1200 seat hall, filled for the "free-but-ticket-only" concert, blunted her physical discomforts but hardly the challenge of the 6,000 ft. altitude, where blowing was difficult and tiring.

Rand Daily Mail News, 2 November 1971
Can the audience be blamed for their reaction when Elaine Shaffer lifted her flute to play the opening statement of the Mozart G major Concerto? Not having seen or heard a woman flute virtuoso before, many of them broke into nervous giggles that obviously implied not the slightest disrespect for the soloist. It was only a minority in the audience that later found a rapid run to an emphatic top note on the flute so unexpected and startling as to be funny.

Traditionally, African men rather than African women are musicians, and the brio of a cadenza played by a woman was a totally new and almost embarrassing experience.

Applause at the end of the performance, however, left no doubt as to the sincerity of the audience's appreciation of playing which was, if anything, better than the standard of the same work and the same soloist at the SABC symphony concert a few days earlier.

By comparison with Soweto audiences which regularly get SABC symphony concerts, the Boi Ketlong listeners were unsophisticated in their musical tastes and so, not surprisingly, found a four-movement symphony rather long in its demands on their powers of concentration. No white audience attending a symphony concert of this type for the first time could have been better behaved.

The following morning, Elaine delighted in the opportunity to enjoy the intimacy of Bantu school children. They gathered close, curious to view the American woman, attentive as she demonstrated the mechanics of the flute.

Johannesburg
October 31, 1971
On October 22nd the President of the Radio Company (our sponsor) gave an official lunch because Efi told him it was my birthday. We both received presents. Efi got gold cuff links and I a gold brooch with tiger's eye (semi-precious stone) in the middle.

We have been feeling tired, probably because of the extra effort needed for this altitude. We made a big effort to refuse all the invitations to homes to relax. Instead we stay in the hotel, really relaxing. They are hospitable and sweet, but I can't sit anymore after the 23 hour plane ride.

The Star, Johannesburg, 27 October 1971
Elaine Shaffer is a flautist of the finest caliber and a true artist. Her technique is awe-inspiring, her tone very beautiful, and her breath control in a lengthy passage is phenomenal. The opening movement of Mozart's Flute Concerto No. 1 in G Major, K. 313 was played with bright and translucent tone, the feather-light runs and trills of the cadenza being quite remarkable.

Chalet Mandi II
Gstaad
November 24, 1971
Dear Beverly,
South Africa already seems far away—no, I would <u>not</u> like to live there. It is a Fascist police state, and one is always in danger of arrest. You probably read of the Anglican Dean of Johannesburg. Five years sentence only for helping the families of political prisoners with food, clothing, etc. They arrested 100 people within 3 wks. and use torture methods. It is not only the blacks that are badly treated (low wages, etc.) but now the whites as well. A Christian there who speaks out will now be in danger of arrest. And a genuine Christian <u>must</u> be against the government.

However, as for the music, the last review for Efi in Johannesburg had the headline: <u>Kurtz The Best Guest</u>, referring to his reception compared to others in recent years, including Sir Thomas Beecham, Malcolm Sargent, Dorati, etc.

My personal treasure from South Africa was the gift of black circular earrings made of gold and elephant hair!

A Legacy of Recordings

Elaine first ventured into recording with London's His Master's Voice (HMV) and the two Mozart Concertos, with Efrem Kurtz conducting the Philharmonia Orchestra. The intricacies of recording technology created new and different demands for perfection. Less than superb results could shadow artistic success. Elaine became familiar with the recording studio as an interested onlooker during many of Efrem's sessions. The long intense hours, imprisoned in a sterile control room, listening to every note, critiquing and adjusting, tried her nerves. Playbacks never fully pleased her, knowing imperfections usually must be accepted as indelible.

I never wanted to make records, but with the new director of His Master's Voice, Mr. Olaf, I could do it. He has the kind of sympathetic attitude that is necessary <u>and</u> he knows music. They want me to record both Mozart Concertos now. The new assistant to Olaf is a flute player who thinks no one exists but me and wants to do the whole repertoire.

Le Pavillon
Gstaad
11 November 1957

Dear Daddie Rex,
    At the moment, the main thing on my mind is the coming recordings. It is a tremendous task, and I want to do the very best, but the more one reaches for perfection, the more elusive it becomes. I have 4 different editions of the music, 3 different existing recordings (all bad) and my tape recorder and am taking the music apart as if I never knew it, even tho' I have performed it 30 times in public. It is a great challenge and there is always some fear and apprehension associated with

the unknown, this being my first experience. One thing is reassuring, to have a sympathetic conductor (!) and the head artistic director of HMV is also a kind man, so no one to get on my nerves in any way. We have 9 hrs. to make 26 min. of music. I am working a lot on perfecting technique because perfection is actually more important than expression in recording, esp. in these HI-FI times.

Ritz Hotel
London
26 November 1957

Dear Mother and Daddie Rex,
Just want to tell you that the recording went superbly. I was in excellent form, and everyone was happy at HMV. I am getting a long contract, and they feel they have made a "great discovery."
I haven't written as I have an inflamed tendon in my wrist from working too much (scraping the music with a little knife).

Ritz Hotel
Dec. 9, 1957

Dearest Family,
This is the only chance to get a word to you for Christmas. We just finished a session of recording and it was difficult because of not feeling well. At this point I want to forget the recording and forget about music for at least a week. Efi says he's going to hide the flute, or send it via rocket around the earth.
(Incidentally, did you hear of the 2 Russian scientists who knocked at the door of heaven and said, "We don't want to get in—we just came to get our ball back.")

LePavillon
Christmas Eve
1957

Dear Daddie Rex and Mother,
Some artists are good for records, but I'm sure I will never make a good one. I can't stand the mechanical atmosphere.

*Most of all, I miss not having an audience. "Just a show-off"
I guess.
I almost "cracked up" the last 10 days in London. The
orchestra was nice, and sympathetic when everything seemed
to go to pieces. I even fell <u>up</u> the stairs that day <u>with</u> the golden
flute in right hand—not a scratch on the flute, amazingly,
but a black and blue knee and stiff left arm. I have to spend
2 days sorting out with the engineer at HMV boxes of many
attempts. I am almost recovered from the experience, though
still see red lights and hear Mozart in my sleep!*

WOLFGANG AMADEUS MOZART

Elaine's recordings are 33 LPs, at first monophonic. The titles are listed,
using wording and comments from the covers.

**Mozart—Elaine Shaffer—The Two Concertos for
Flute and Orchestra and the Andante in C—The
Philharmonia Orchestra, Efrem Kurtz conducting.
Concerto No.1 in G Major K 313
Concerto No. 2 in D Major K313
Elaine Shaffer, flute with The Philharmonia Orchestra,
Efrem Kurtz conducting.**
[EMI Capital and Seraphim Series both issued this work.]
"Mozart apologizes for the incomplete work due to
constraints of time and his powerlessness when obliged
to write for an instrument which he could not bear! The
music in these concertos is hardly evidence of his apologie."
(Deryck Cooke: notes)

These Mozart concertos, listed in the March 6, 1960 Sunday edition
of the *New York Herald Tribune,* carried a large photo and a review.
The Records column of the April *New York Times* named the recording
among its Recent Choice Disks, along with Heifetz, Horowitz and other
respectable names.

JOHANN SEBASTIAN BACH

Elaine was soloist with members of the Bath Festival Orchestra during its festival in 1959. Collaboration and friendship with Yehudi Menuhin initiated the remarkable Bach recordings. *The Brandenburg Concerto*, Bach *Suite No. 2* and *The Musical Offering* gathered rave reviews and was acclaimed as "a major artistic achievement" and "it knocks all of its competitors out of the ring."

Bach The Musical Offering, Yehudi Menuhin with members of the Bach Festival Orchestra and Elaine Shaffer, (flute)
"The deeply felt performances given here show how the music has affected the performers . . . and the recorded sound, especially in stereo, is remarkably lifelike." *(The Gramophone)*

The Complete Brandenburg Concertos No. 5 in D (with George Malcolm), Suite No. 2
Musical Offering with Yehudi Menuhin and the Bath Festival Orchestra
The Four Suites for Orchestra, Yehudi Menuhin conducting the Bath Festival Chamber Orchestra with Elaine Shaffer, flute.
Suite No. 1 in C Major BWV.1066
Suite No. 2 in B Minor BWV.1067
Suite No. 3 in D Major BWV.1068
Suite No. 4 in D Major BWV.1069
"The spiritual insight and musical mastery that Menuhin and colleagues brought to the Brandenburgs last year is now applied to the four orchestral suites and the result is equally impressive, in some ways even more so." (Denis Stevens in *The Gramophone*)

The B Minor is written for strings, harpsichord and solo flute. Elaine shines in the lively, playful Badinerie, sometimes used as an encore.

J. S. Bach's Orchestral Suites and Concertos was produced in 1982, reissued as a boxed set of CDs with interesting notes. "In 1959 the Brandenburg Concertos were not only performed live at the Bath Festival and broadcast by the BBC but recorded by EMI. In the Fifth the solo harpsichord was played by George Malcolm and the flute by the enchanting American player, Elaine Shaffer. In 1960 Menuhin and the Bath Festival Orchestra turned to the Orchestral Suites, with Shaffer returning to play the important part in the Second Suite."

> *Grand Hotel e La Pace*
> *Montecatini Terme, Italy*
> *June 17, 1960*

Dear Mother & Daddie Rex,
(Using carbon copy system)
  The recording sessions went very well. Everyone was pleased, including Yehudi, musicians in orchestra, and engineers. We listen to play backs on stereo now. I like the sound of the flute better on stereo, but it seems to give an unnatural reproduction as a whole. For instance, in a concert one would hardly hear the harpsichord, and in stereo it is magnified to equal the balance of other instruments. Certain listeners complain about live performances and say they are not as good as recorded versions!
  The day before we started I went to Yehudi's home to practice with him, and afterwards was very upset, as his interpretation was so different in every way from mine. I even thought of giving up the whole thing. But once the sessions started he began to slowly come over to my interpretation, and in the end, it is almost as I would have wanted it. (He didn't know the Bach Suite and was copying the ideas from a <u>bad</u> recording.)
  Have you heard the <u>Brandenburg No. 5</u> that we did last year? It should be released by now on Capitol. Critics say it is the best in existence.

Bach Flute Sonatas Sonata in B Minor, BWV.1030 A Major BWV.1032 and E Minor BMV.1034 Vol. 1.
"The B minor is unquestionably the finest of Bach's instrumental works for flute and is 'large' in every sense.

The first movement is one of Bach's supreme creations! Bach's composition shows total disregard for the wind player's need to breathe, let alone the necessity of resting the lips, but displays a quite extraordinary (and at this time unique) understanding of the instrument's emotional range." (Charles Enderby: notes 1965)

Bach Flute Sonatas with George Malcolm, Harpsichord, and Ambrose Gauntlett, Viola Da Gamba Vol. 2.

"The E Major deserves special attention because of the emotionally high-charged opening and the graceful canon which comprises the third movement." (C. Enderby: notes 1966)

"Triumphant Performances of the Bach Flute Sonatas" is headlined in the Best of the Month in *Hi/Fi Stereo Review*, August 1966.

"The playing on this set (Angel recording) is little short of miraculous. Her playing is totally relaxed, superbly rhythmic, and anything but mechanically metronomic. Her melodic lines tend to float over the pulse and across the bar lines in a way few solo musicians ever achieve. Her ornaments are scrupulously correct, her breath control completely up to the almost impossible demands of the music and her tone something far too beautiful to come out of a length of pipe. She is a superb musician." (James Goodfriend)

MOZART AND TELEMANN

Mozart Concerto in C Major for Flute, Harp and Orchestra (with Marilyn Costello), Yehudi Menuhin Conducting
Telemann Suite in A Minor for Flute and Strings, The Philharmonia Orchestra, conducted by Yehudi Menuhin

Old Beach Hotel
Monte Carlo
9 July 1963

Dear Mother and Daddie Rex,
Re: Mozart with Marilyn Costello
    Yehudi did a marvelous job—he is such a great musician. He had trouble sometimes with the actual technique of conducting, but his ideas were marvelous. At one point he couldn't make the orchestra play together, was trying different ways, then called to Efrem in the control room, "Efrem, what should I do?"
    There is a new man, a wonderful musician, at HMV who will put all the pieces together of the record. I trust him and will be relieved of the torture of having to listen and help choose the best bits. Efi says it's a <u>great</u> record. I really don't know—the only thing I'm sure of, both Mozart and Telemann are better than any <u>existing</u> records. You will be surprised at how different my Telemann is from Kincaid's.
    Marilyn played beautifully. That was part of the pressure on me, that I suggested her to HMV. I think they want to make more records with her. As for me, HMV wants to record all the 8 Bach Sonatas (later 12 Handel Sonatas). That will be a job! Travel upsets things. I can cope as long as there is peace and time to work.

St. Moritz
Palace Hotel
15 August 1963

Dearest Beverly and Aaron, (carbon)
    <u>The artistic director of HMV</u> *wrote to us the following, "The Mozart and Telemann is excellent, a really great record—so musical and splendid playing all round. Please let me tell you that I am not exaggerating if I say it is one of the finest musical performances—and I reckon to be pretty hard boiled. I had the tapes put together by my dear friend J.W. who is a first class musician and who enjoyed it thoroughly."*

The output and machinations of the recordings of Mozart and Bach which Elaine and Yehudi Menuhin produced would test any relationship. It secured their respect for each others' musicianship as well as their friendship. (In 1959, after playing chamber music together in each other's home in Gstaad, he intimated to Efrem that he would like to take months off to study with Elaine.)

Gstaad
20 April, 1964
Dear Beverly,
*   This is to me somewhat like the Dogmatics (theology) are to Barth, the highest goal, to try to do Bach justice. Sometimes the whole thing seems overwhelming. But the harpsichordist is* <u>*great*</u>*, and is in himself an inspiration.*

Gstaad
29 April 1964
Dear Daddie Rex and Mother,
*   Try to remember me on May 5, 6, 7, 8, 9—the days of recording. The more I study Bach the less I know—the whole task seems overwhelming. I'm only glad I didn't do the recordings 10 years ago—maybe it would be better to wait 10 years more before doing them!*

London
10 May 1964
Dear Mother,
*   My marathon is mostly finished—5 days from 9 to 6—but I didn't get everything done, and have 2 more sessions. It was a real strain physically and emotionally, but it went rather smoothly, the surroundings were pleasant—everyone was helpful and encouraging. They all think it will be a great record. One thing I am pleased about is I believe they have this time finally captured my real sound and not a flat, colorless, imitation.*
*   HMV has more plans of things for me to record. Actually I have done 2 LPs (7 sonatas for Flute and Harpsichord) and 2/3 of another LP, including the Bach* <u>*Solo*</u> *Sonata and a trio of Bach for 2 flutes and harpsichord—I am recording*

both flute parts—it was my idea. (I do get a good idea once in 10 years!)
Have recorded the 1ˢᵗ flute part with the harpsichord, and will do the second part while listening simultaneously to the other part through a loudspeaker, turned on softly near my ear. It will be a tricky business but interesting. Besides it is impossible to find a flute player in Europe who would match my sound, so it will be more successful this way.

KUHLAU, SCHUBERT, F. X. MOZART

ELAINE SHAFFER—flute
HEPHZIBAH MENUHIN—piano
KUHLAU: Flute Sonata in E Minor Op 71
SCHUBERT: Introduction & Variation of "Trockne Blumen" D 802 Op 160
FRANZ XAVIER MOZART: Rondo in E Minor
Kuhlau (1786-1832) son of a German military bandsman became a Danish citizen. He was appointed to the service of the king, playing the flute in the court orchestra, and wrote an enormous quantity of music for the flute.
Schubert (1797-1828) wrote this variation on his own song, Torckne Blumen, for flautist Ferdinand Bogner, a music professor in Vienna. "They are said to be virtuostic in character and say a great deal for the professor and his pianist—and for Elaine and Hephzibah."
Mozart (1791-1844) Franz Xavier, the sixth child of Mozart, was hesitant to produce anything under his genius father. Elaine ends this recital recording with the Rondo in E Minor where Franz X proves himself able to compose something unique. (Excerpts R. Golding: notes)

DANZI

This delightful recording with the Paris Philharmonic is unpublished and in my personal collection as a LP recording done live during its performance in Paris. This may be the work Elaine discovered in Berlin, after a conversation with Stokowski when he challenged her to "find something other than Kuhlau."

AARON COPLAND

Aaron Copland's Duo for Flute and Piano (1970-71) commissioned by a group of pupils and admirers of the late William Kincaid, is dedicated to his memory. Elaine first performed the Duo on October 3, 1971 at Philadelphia's Settlement Music School, with Hephzibah Menuhin as pianist.

Duo for Flute and Piano, Elaine Shaffer, Flutist, Aaron Copland, Pianist. Masterwork Dept. of CBC Records included this work in a recording **"Copland Performs and Conducts Copland."**

Aaron Copland writes about the composition in his biography, Copland/Since 1943. *"Duo for Flute and Piano* is in three movements, with indications . . . the second movement has a certain mood that I connect with myself—a rather sad and wistful one, I suppose. Being aware that many of the flutists who were responsible for commissioning the piece would want to play it, I tried to make it grateful for the performer, but no amateur could handle the Duo—it requires a good player. When Elaine and I rehearsed for the Columbia recording of Duo, I missed several of my own notes, but Elaine just smiled sweetly and missed none at all!"

FRENCH FLUTE PASSION

Flute-Passion is a 2 CD set released in 2002 by French EMI. It included an earlier recording of Bach Suite No. 2 with Elaine and the Bath Festival Orchestra, with Yehudi Menuhin. (The French are known to misspell Shaffer as "Schaffer.")

Elaine's music remains as audio tapes, CDs and re-mastered CDs, a gift that validates so much of the vivid expressions in reviews and articles. Critics at times seemed stretched for a vocabulary to bring to life an experience that took audiences to another place. Her unique tone, phrasing, breath-control, and technical mastery survive in the recordings.

Mountain Wedding: Mountain Home

The seamstress in Nice admired Elaine's choice of an exquisite, simple white dress, a Jacques Fath design. "It looks like it could be for a wedding," she said. Yes, it was the wedding dress. Elaine Shaffer and Efrem Kurtz settled on August 15, 1955 for their marriage ceremony in St. Moritz, Switzerland. Elaine owned her uncertainties and struggles that had kept the wedding in flux.

> *Selsdon Park, Surrey*
> *June 3, 1954*
>
> *Dear Mother,*
> *I probably will not get married for awhile. There are some complications and I don't want to be sorry later. It is only me who is holding it up, so don't blame Efrem.*

Much was happening for both Elaine and Efrem in their world of music. He had a successful conducting and recording reputation in Europe. Her schedule kept her involved while preparing for proposed engagements and her career. Reports of their European travels and performances confirmed the unwavering depth of their love. They seemed an enviable match.

Efrem maintained his role as "the maestro" over the years I knew him. His suave magic directed a choice table from the maitre d'. Guests were breathless when he engineered not only the seating and the menu, but then laid out the next day's activities and meal plans. Elaine caught his attention in Kansas City when she came from Philadelphia with a unique talent and ambitious dedication. She confessed to taking her time to evaluate him as conductor. She had never listened to his recordings and rated him "above average" until eventually, with strong conviction, she placed him among the great ones.

Elaine's classic beauty blossomed after the summer in California. She became fit, fashionably slim and healthy. She retained the characteristic dimple and clear blue eyes. A colorful chiffon scarf regularly held the light brown hair of her pony tail. The attractive, simple fashion she favored remained current even in photographs of later years.

An elusive aura, an essential dimension of Elaine's person proved to be other than physical. An aspect of her devout faith radiated. As a Christian she had fallen in love and now wanted to marry her Jewish conductor.

Efrem was not known to practice his Jewish beliefs by attendance at synagogue or observance of high holy days. He took note of Elaine's habit of regular attendance at church. When he questioned a change in her routine, she reminded him, *"I cannot go to church since you schedule rehearsals on Sunday."* One day at Elaine's invitation, they tuned the radio to listen together to a sermon of Billy Graham, broadcast from The White House. Efrem later attributed that message to a lingering inspiration that affected his conducting. *It shows in the music. Last night was a really great performance of the Beethoven Fifth. The manager of the orchestra came in the dressing room after and broke down, he was overcome; also others were affected. You know what kind of music it takes to do that.*

Efrem clearly understood the main stumbling blocks that delayed their marriage.

Sanderstead, Surrey
June 3, 1954

Dear Beverly,

There are real problems which I can't truthfully say are new ones. I want to write to you and see what your and Aaron's reactions are.

After a long discussion, Efrem told me that there are really two reasons why I am not completely sure. One is: the question of the difference of religion. He said that the only way to answer it would be if he would become a Christian, and he can't do that because he would be denying what he really is. This is a strong point, since he was brought up in the Orthodox faith, although he never goes to the Synagogue now. He knows religion is more important to me than to him, but he respects it, and has no prejudice.

The second reason he gave for my indecision was the relationship with his ex-wife. He gets many letters from her, which he does not try to hide, but always tells me there is little more than friendly chit-chat—that there is nothing to do with love in their relationship, but that he will always be her friend, and always help her when she needs it. He thinks I will eventually change in my attitude to this.

There is also another side to this story. I know more than anyone what he has done for me, how much he really loves me, and he would be completely lost without me. In truth, he is a perfect choice for a husband.

I hope you will write me immediately to the Savoy. I am writing because you have been here and known Efrem quite well, so perhaps you have observations which can be of some assistance.

Countless discussions over time on the history and messages of the Bible assured Elaine that Efrem understood the depth of her faith, as he honored his own. She was *ready to overlook the less-than-perfect part.* Their marriage surely brought peace and true happiness to them both.

Switzerland was a choice setting for the wedding. The Alpine beauty of the village of St. Moritz made it a picturesque site. Also there were fond memories of Elaine's summers of successful performances at the Engadine Festival.

Palace Hotel
9 August 1955

Dear Bev and Aaron,

You have probably heard about my white dress—then I have white shoes, white hat, and white satin gloves, above the elbow. I am really getting excited—the strange thing is that everything seems so right now—the time, etc. I am not at all doubtful, as so often before when I thought of marriage. I have never been so happy in my life—I only wish you could be here to share it!

Oh, almost forgot. I was surprised to receive a beautiful diamond ring—it belonged to Efi's mother. It suits my hand so well. One stone, in an old-fashioned high setting, and a white gold band—the wedding ring is a plain gold band the same size, only in yellow gold.

The burgomaster is a wonderful man—he will perform the civil ceremony and then we will have prayers by Bob [our brother] and Pastor Schulthess. Herbert will be the other witness and perhaps Laila, or Mrs. Berry, wife of the physician and a good friend.

St. Moritz
Switzerland
15 August 1955

Dearest Mother and Dad and Pat,

How I wish you could all be here—first for the beautiful scenery and second for the wedding. We could not have chosen a more perfect place in the whole world! Bob is already on top of the mountain (10,000 ft.). Yesterday I had a wonderful walk with him (4 hours)—you would all be so happy to see him as he is now—he looks absolutely handsome, strong and happy.

We are having a reception for about 40 people in the hotel, and at 4:20 will take the train to Lucerne, stay there 3 days and then go to Montreux to look for a house somewhere between there and Lausanne.

Palace Hotel
Lucerne
18 August 1955

Dearest Mother and Dad,

We have the beautiful bridal suite overlooking the lake. I want to say I recommend marriage. We kept saying it wouldn't be any different from before, but it is. I feel wonderful, and our honeymoon is perfect. Such a peaceful feeling—I was silly to worry about it before! Did you see the <u>World Telegram</u> (N.Y.)—"internationally famous flutist E. S. married the conductor E. Kurtz in St. Moritz, etc." Efi says he is jealous that my name is first.

A German newspaper highlighted that summer's residents in St. Moritz: "Distinguished guests, Lady Winston Churchill, her daughter Mary Soames-Churchill, golf champion Harry Cotton, the conductor,

Efrem Kurtz and the <u>famous</u> flutist, Elaine Shaffer." Efrem enjoyed his own rephrasing, "the stinker Kurtz, but the <u>famous</u> E. S."

They were content to remain in the areas of Montreux, Lausanne and Lucerne while Efrem went each day for treatment of maladies of the arm and shoulder. These locations appealed as possibilities for real estate, weighing the climate, proximity to airports or major highways. Life in hotels had lost its charm and married life spurred them to begin a serious search for their own "chateau."

Mountain Home

Park Hotel
Gstaad
18 September 1955

Dear Family,
How I wish you could all be here now. It is where I came after my operation last year, about 4500 ft. high, and surrounded by mountains, all covered with snow. Just a few days ago the ground was all covered too, now the sun is shining, blue sky and it is just a dream.

Elaine was about to fall in love once more, this time with a tiny village in the narrow valley of the Bernese Oberland. In Gstaad she used "Paradise" to describe her sense of this "home." She returned whenever possible and found solace after an exhausting season of performance and travel. The Christmas-village setting with its range of mountains on each side befriended her as she crossed the flower-covered bridge on the way to the bakery early in the morning. A shortcut through the pine woods bypassed the busy streets, especially in tourist season. *I feel safe here. I could walk these woods at midnight and never fear.*

Le Pavillon became the chalet where they eventually consolidated their belongings and experienced a semblance of permanency. The picturesque cottage used Swiss regulated architecture: weathered wood with balconies that opened to window boxes bursting with geraniums. It sat high in a meadow dotted with cows, their tinkling bells breaking the delicious mountain silence.

The owner of the chalet was Rebekah Harkness, widow of William Hale Harkness, one of the founders of Standard Oil Company. This property in Gstaad no longer held an interest for Mrs. Harkness. There were homes in New York City, Nassau, Watch Hill, and elsewhere, where philanthropic affairs occupied her.

Mrs. Harkness returned to Gstaad, surprisingly, for her own marriage in the village. Elaine and Efrem spent their first Christmas as husband and wife with the Harkness family in a newly-purchased chalet which Mrs. Harkness refurbished with lavish colors. The friendship continued with only sporadic contact, while Elaine and Efrem lovingly cared for Le Pavillon as their only home, the place of precious respites, always too brief. Here they found contentment as they beautified the gardens, mowed the grass, planted bulbs, and satisfied Elaine's domestic urges denied her in hotels.

> *Le Pavillon*
> *Gstaad*
> *13 October, 1959*

Dear Mother,

What a joy to be in our hide-away (Gstaad). In our life so little time to stop and reflect on what we are doing, what has been done, and to look into the future. This is the perfect peace which restores the body and sort of slows down the motor for a short time.

I am on the balcony and the sun is really hot though there was a heavy frost last night. The cows are all down from the high mountains now, so the sound of their bells is in the background. Next to our lot there are sheep grazing. There is something friendly about cows and we don't see them from about June to October. Now they will eat the grass outside until it gets too cold, and then go in the barns for the winter.

Today is one of those heavenly ones; for two days it rained and when it cleared today all of the high mountains are covered with snow. With the sun shining on it and the green of the fields and pine trees—I wish you could see it. It could be easy to take this all for granted; I hope I never do.

The only complaint I have about life is that it is going by too quickly. But at the same time it means that in a short while I can be seeing the family again. In this Space Age we are really not very far apart after all.

Elaine wanted to share a taste of the life she relished, and so invited me to Switzerland for an unforgettable two-week visit. She chose the fall when Efrem was off to conduct in South Africa. I might have chosen the high ski season until Elaine advised me of its dramatic change of pace once crowds of international tourists descended. *"Their jewels match their stylish ski clothes!"*

The winding mountain roads from the Geneva airport were familiar to Elaine as she piloted her little Mercedes convertible. Taking twists and turns for nearly three hours, the picturesque village, with a scattering of toy dwellings, came into view. Will my stomach ever recover? Elaine prescribed peppermint tea, a soothing remedy, as we pulled up to her mountain home.

Day-long hikes nearby began as we climbed the Eggli Mountain. At that altitude, I welcomed a pause for lunch. We leaned our backs against the sunny warmth of a barn, and found meadow rocks to set our delicious beef tongue sandwiches and fresh apple juice. Several hours, following a well-kept trail, took us to the Geltenhutte where we added our names to its log. Days earlier Efrem entered his own favorite comment: "Been here twice, the first and last time."

We browsed the center of the village where Elaine identified her favorite shops. Shopkeepers greeted her as a native, calling her "mountain goat" for her familiarity with the distant peaks. I biked to have a look at a village schoolhouse while Elaine kept to her daily practice schedule.

We dined one evening on a specialty of blue trout, fresh from the mountain restaurant fish tank. It was a delectable delicacy, served with the traditional plain boiled potatoes. One cup of coffee taught me the effect of caffeine in these mountains, keeping me wide-awake that night.

The steady clang of cowbells paved the way as the animals ambled down from the mountain before the long winter season. Sturdy women with weathered complexions took to the center of the road while traffic waited. This scene against the cloudless blue sky and the lingering snow on the highest mountains, a world away, allured "discriminating people" who discovered Gstaad.

The economist, John Kenneth Galbreath, came to the valley the same year as Elaine and Efrem and named residents: Randall Thomson, the composer, William F. Buckley, Jr., political columnist, and Yehudi Menuhin. He overlooked mention of Julie Andrews, Elizabeth Taylor, and the skiing visits of Jackie Kennedy. He wrote this in <u>A Contemporary Guide to Economics, Peace and Laughter</u>. Also: "Efrem Kurtz, the conductor and

Elaine Shaffer Kurtz, the world's best and best looking flutist, live over on another shoulder in a house they rent from Rebekah Harkness which is called naturally The Pavillon."

Elaine accepted and reciprocated few invitations, but often she and Efrem exchanged dinner parties with John Kenneth Galbreath. His provocative conversation made him a lively guest as he offered his self-described "radical liberal views." He appeared at the door of the Pavillon for casual stopovers whenever he chose to be in Gstaad, working on writing projects. He made certain to seat Elaine by Jacqueline Kennedy at a celebrated dinner in Gstaad.

A scheduled performance in Milan, Italy, took us away from all that enchanted me about this other world. A sleek, efficient train swept us from pastoral Switzerland to the bustle of Milan. Crossing the border, Elaine alerted me to the once-over glares of the Italian ticket agent as he moved down the aisle. "Today we are women; no longer cows." We laughed. We were sisters again, delighting in mutual pleasures in nature and music, exploring mountain paths, sharing stories of our family and our different life's journey.

The Kincaid Platinum Flute

William Kincaid played a Powell platinum flute throughout his long career with the Philadelphia Orchestra. The prized instrument was uniquely created for him. During his last illness he passed it to Elaine.

Elaine checked in with her teacher whenever her European concert tour allowed a visit to America, a delightful time for both of them to exchange news from the musical world. Kincaid's mandatory retirement at age 65 ended his familiar place with the orchestra. Instead, from his apartment he watched the comings and goings of his colleagues over at the Academy of Music, his vitality and keen intellect intact. It wasn't until inactivity, melancholy, and the death of his wife, dimmed his zest for life.

The poignant bedside scene, witnessed by Mr. Kincaid's caring nurse, Margaret, indicated that he wanted Elaine to have the flute. Margaret lifted it from the closet shelf knowing he was no longer able to breathe into it that glorious sound. Sometimes he lovingly handled the flute when she brought it to him.

Elaine wrote to a friend of the ordeal that followed:

15 October 1967

Dear Paola, [Soffiotti]

We may come to USA for Christmas . . . but not sure. William Kincaid gave me his platinum flute last Christmas week, but I didn't take it to Japan, as I thought it meant so much to him, it would cause him to "give up" when he already had lost interest in life. The result is, his lawyer, also executor of the estate, will not recognize the gift (even though his nurse was a witness) and insists on a court trial. It may be in Dec. or April. The whole thing is silly and unnecessary but I feel it is worth fighting for what is right. The flute is valued at $3,000 and the total estate was half a million *dollars. Such is life—one does what one feels to be right and sometimes one loses, and the ruthless people go ahead. Even after seeing all the difficulties, I still would not have had the heart to take his flute from him at that time.*

On September 25, 1968 the flute was finally placed in her hands at The Barclay Hotel in Philadelphia. Foregoing a court trial, Elaine forwarded an abundance of documentation to clarify her circumscribed relationship with her teacher, mentor and friend. Yes, the lawyer finally determined that the flute belonged to "Kincaid's foremost disciple."

The *Philadelphia Evening Bulletin* announced the decision with a large photograph of Elaine with the flute. A conversation in an interview with the paper's Adolph Katz spoke of her familiarity with the instrument with quotes from their conversation.

"It was made by Verne Q. Powell of Boston, for the metals exhibition at the fair. I think it was really manufactured with Mr. Kincaid in mind. He bought it after the fair closed. It is still engraved with the Trylon and Perisphere which was the theme of the fair.

"Its value? No one can put a value on it. It was one of the first platinum flutes ever made. But what makes it more important is that it belonged to such a great artist.

"An instrument seems to take on the personality of the person who plays it and takes his name. I suppose the value of the Kincaid flute can be compared to the value of a Stradivarius violin.

"This flute will continue to bear the Kincaid name no matter who owns it, long after me."

"There is a slight difference in tone between a silver and platinum flute, but it really depends on how it is played. A platinum flute does not change as much as silver with changes in temperature. The pitch does not vary with the temperature."

Finally she spoke of the friendship of nearly 25 years, attesting to their deep and lasting mutual regard for her only teacher. **"I used to visit him quite often."**

Philadelphia heard the publicized flute at the world premiere of Aaron Copland's *Duo for Flute and Piano* on October 3, 1971. Elaine performed this work, commissioned in honor of the memory of William Kincaid and his 40 years as eminent principal flute with the Philadelphia Orchestra. Hepzibah Menuhin, renowned pianist and colleague of Elaine, collaborated on this auspicious occasion at the Settlement Music School. William Kincaid began his Philadelphia teaching career at the school before joining the Curtis Institute. Sol Schoenbach, formerly of the Philadelphia Orchestra, performed as a bassoonist in a Beethoven trio. Aaron Copland enjoyed the occasion to personally thank many contributors to this living memorial, his *Duo for Flute and Piano*.

John Solum initiated the commission for the Copland work and played a major part in soliciting funds. Former students and friends of Kincaid responded, led by Eugene Ormandy and Leopold Stokowski. A New York premiere followed at Hunter College Playhouse on October 9, 1971 with the same performers.

Columbia Records produced the recording of Copland's composition with Elaine playing the platinum flute and Aaron Copland at the piano. Brief notes in their correspondence arranged for rehearsal sessions to take place at Copland's suburban New York home. The imposing piano sat before expansive windows, creating a picture of a woodland setting. It was not the last time Elaine played the flute.

Note: The flute's final acquisition is a historical mystery. Christie's received it for auction from Efrem Kurtz on October 18, 1986. Collector S. Pivar, the highest bidder, loaned it to be displayed at The Metropolitan Museum of Art, New York, NY. Subsequently it was removed to be auctioned once more on October 13, 2009.

Time is Too Short
1969-70

Elaine took to heart Chagall's words, "You must always work." He spoke them in the summer of 1969. As if a mantra, Elaine's career had always been <u>work</u>. In these later years her pace of travel and scheduled performances accelerated, with evidence of an unimaginable output of high quality work.

> *Antibes*
> *July 20, 1969*
> *Had dinner with Chagalls the night before leaving. Chagall asked me to play and I hadn't practiced—he said 'one should always work.' He works every day here when he is supposed to be on vacation at 83 years.*

> *July 22, 1970*
> *He has a strong feeling of time being short and has so much he wants to do. He is working all the time. His memory is astounding and his reactions are those of a young man. I am practicing because of what he told me last year, 'you must always work.'*

"Time is too short," a haunting expression, used by Elaine unknowingly in her last years. Her gracious friendship and collaboration with Hephzibah Menuhin brought new depth and urgency to her professional life. They had first met at dinner at the home of Yehudi Menuhin. Hephzibah was an established gifted pianist, ideally partnered with Elaine. The musical affinity of these two women attracted new audiences while each one accommodated a solo career. For them, a common bond, an understanding of the soul of music, was sensed by adoring audiences. Reviews from one concert spoke of **a program (that) unfolded with extreme purity of sound, and complete spiritual accord, with passionate "élan" and rigorous style. Shaffer and Menuhin gave brilliant performances. Very warm applause from the crowded hall.** *V Corriere della Sera,* Milan, 28 Jan. 1970

Elaine sympathized whenever Hephzibah's conversations veered from music to deep compassion for the ills of society. Married to Richard Hauser, an English sociologist, she lived in a derelict district of London where cab drivers feigned familiarity. Both husband and wife were devoted to a program that reached out to those caught in addiction and poverty. That life contrasted her profession, Hephzibah said, so that it made music-making easy. Her performances combined an expression of beauty, clouded with the needs of humanity. In a receiving line, following a concert, a patron complimented, "You so inspired me." "And what did I inspire you to do?" Hephzibah responded.

A video-taped interview (conversation between pieces of music) after their Jan. 26, 1969 concert in Paris:

> *At the interview we hoped to create a 'live' atmosphere. Then Gavaty asked me how I came to play the flute. I said I really wanted to play football, but the nearest thing was the marching band. It broke them all up. So that humor helped, along with Hephzibah saying she would have liked to be the wife of Beethoven.*
>
> *I spoke in French (after telling the producer I would speak in English with a translator). Hephzibah speaks perfect French and she spoke for ½ hour answering questions of the moderator. He was in tears—it was all very moving, almost a miracle to create in that cold, hardly functioning studio. (Rostropovich and Milstein were the last artists included in this video series.)*
>
> *Hephzibah is so good to be with both musically and otherwise. She is a great woman and the association with her has enriched my life enormously.*

A graphic reminder epitomized Elaine's *work* in four volumes of the scrapbooks that preserved her reviews. News clippings from August 1959 to June 1971 of more than fifty different international performances were neatly taped on oversized pages with many reviews in the native language, some translated to English.

Ten concerts, nine cities, four countries, all within five weeks in 1969, certainly spoke of an impressive schedule, until we read between the lines of her unexplained tiredness, discomfort, flu-like illnesses and later incapacitating pain. The water or mud treatments prescribed at famous health spas in Montecatini, Ischia, or Godesburg brought only temporary relief. Elaine's cherished remedy was long walks or bike rides in the invigorating air of Switzerland, essential to sustain her lung power and energy.

> *Walked to Turbach and took the bus back. Took the train to Lenk and walked back to Gstaad, over the Wassengrat (3½ hrs.). Biked from Gstaad to Chateau d' O'ex, 19 miles.*

> *10 February 1969*
> *Am working on the Neilson <u>Concerto</u> for 4 performances in Denmark. I have never done it and the Danes know it like their National Anthem. I have it memorized. Listened to two "bad" American recordings, and one Danish flutist. I can do better.*

> *Hotel Angleterre*
> *Copenhagen*
> *1 March 1969*
> *Dear Mother,*
> *Before rehearsal I ran for 10 minutes and felt asthmatic afterwards (probably because of bad air on city streets), but it went away, except the burning sensation in the tubes. In the middle of the night I had 101 degrees temp. and next day 102.5 all day. Have been in bed and bronchitis still there, take penicillin, 1 million units a day. Doctor says it is probably Hong Kong flu with complications. First concert is cancelled because the orchestra's major players also hard hit.*

> *March 7, 1969*
> *Neilson <u>Concerto</u> was great hit with raving reviews. His daughter came to the concert and said I recreated the piece. Hasn't been done here for ages. The American Ambassador,*

Angier Biddle Duke sent us flowers. I will also do a recital with pianist Rasmussen.

Berlinske Tidende, Copenhagen, March 6, 1969 (translation)
It was a great pleasure to listen to Elaine Shaffer. In her hands the flute is a capricious instrument, a noble instrument. Her 'legato' passages were of remarkable evenness, of a special mature beauty. Elaine Shaffer seemed to take an active interest in the strange concerto by Carl Neilson, and thus <u>she made it live for the audience.</u>

Naestred, Denmark
3 March 1969

Dear Mother and Daddie Rex,
I finished my bit, now Efi is doing Beethoven 5ᵗʰ. Forgot to mention I have a date with the English Chamber Orchestra Oct. 29, an all-Bach program, George Malcolm as harpsichordist and conductor. To help ticket sales I felt the "urge" to ask Yehudi. Surprise! He accepted. I proposed we would donate profits to his school outside of London for musically gifted children. I'm glad about this development. American Ambassador Annenberg to be guest of honor.

The sold-out performance in London proved to be a gala, even though the ambassador did not attend. Profits for the school were equal to $1,000.

Madrid

Gstaad
12 June 1969

Dear Mother and Daddie Rex,
Madrid was a fantastic success, the most enthusiastic I have ever had. The performance was also exceptional in both concerts. I could do almost everything I intended to do on the stage and was not too nervous. The young Spanish conductor Fruhbeck did a good accompaniment. Of course they were

using my orchestral material, which helped a lot. The first evening Princess Sofia was there and we were presented to her afterwards in a special room. Have a nice photograph with her. (Sister of King Constantine and married to Juan Carlos.)

There were a number of musicians and a conductor from La Scala there as well as our usual friends. The atmosphere was special—they were all like in a trance. On Sunday morning the ovation was even bigger; they stood up and came toward the stage. Seemed like everyone was screaming. They all said it was the greatest success of the season. The husband of Victoria de Los Angeles was there and was out of his mind with enthusiasm. He said he must go on his knees, etc. however, that meant a lot since he is married to such a great singer.

Mother and Dad Visit

In mid September, with the Gstaad Festival over, Mother and Dad came to Switzerland for a second delightful visit. Elaine arranged opportunities to share walks, explore, meet favorite people and enjoy some scheduled performances. Subsequently I found Elaine's wistful letter marked with heavy underlines, possibly added by Mother as she re-read the nostalgic words.

> *Gstaad*
> *2 October, 1969*

Dear Daddie and Mother,

We miss you very much. The time passed too quickly and there was still more to do, more to say—but I suppose that's life—everything must come to an end. I cleaned my studio and put all the clothes in order—put away summer things, etc. until midnight. Otherwise I would have felt too sad! I am working intensely for the concert in Torino.

Sunday we took the lift to the second stop at Diablerets and walked "Daddy's walk" down—it was beautiful—1hr. 5 minutes. We missed you both! We looked across the lake to the walk we took together the Sunday before.

13 October 1969

Dearest Beverly,

Torino concert was a great success and I was almost pleased for a change. All of the climbing (with mother and dad) did help a lot—I felt strong on the legs and lots of breath to spare. Did the whole recital, a difficult one, from memory. Manager didn't expect anyone to come as he said, "People in Torino don't like flute concerts." House was full—he was excited about that, and even more that they really enjoyed it! Review in the most important paper in Italy and in Europe was sensational.

La Stampa, (translated) *Unione Musicale,* Torino, 8 Oct. 1969

No one so far dethroned Elaine Shaffer, that American flutist who inspires sympathy as soon as she appears, by her clear conception, her pure style, and by the communicative cordiality of her music making. (Few are aware of the fact that, in order to play the flute well, one needs a volume of breath similar to that of a 100 yard sprinter: the science of an athlete is needed if they are to play a wind instrument).

Geneva
21 October 1969

Dear Mother and Daddie Rex,

We went for our last walk, up the Winspillen. It was warm and sunny and I lay down on the grass under a tree— the tree had yellow leaves and black branches—that against the sky with the sun shining through was really divine. Then little by little the clouds came, and in about 15 minutes the sky was covered with clouds. So that made it a little easier to leave. Today it is sunny.

Strasbourg went well, though I didn't like the acoustics in the over-heated hall. These recitals are really a strain, and I feel in a mild state of collapse afterwards. We went out with the organizers afterwards until 1 AM, then drove to Zurich next morning at 7.30 (3½ hours through thick fog). Could sleep for an hour before rehearsing three hours that eve with

180

the Zurich Chamber Orchestra. We left at 7 AM for Gstaad through fog again.

The body carried on and Elaine practiced long hours, memorized selected works, and drove the Mercedes SL to rehearsals, performances and medical appointments for herself and Efi.

> *Gstaad*
> *30 Jan. 1970*
>
> *Dear Mother*
>   *I woke with kind of stomach flu, (fever, chills) but with will power drove to Lausanne, (Efi went with me) took train to Milan. Monday fever was gone.*
>   *Concert Tuesday (Milan) went well, considering 2000 people (even stage was full). Reviews raving. Hephzibah went to N. Y. next day and plays 2 times there, then comes back to play with me in Rome next week. I already feel better, keeping very strict diet and trying to sleep.*

Giulio Confalonieri, *Il Giorno,* Milan, 28. 1. 1970 (translated)
The flutist Elaine Shaffer returned to the Ocieta del Quartetto and had another distinguished success. She possesses, first of all, an uncommon gift among virtuosi of the flute: the ability to eliminate metallic and piercing sounds and to produce instead a tone of exceptional warmth with mellowness and roundness.

A Woman Conductor

The excitement of an artistic "first" came as an irresistible invitation for Elaine to conduct in Lisbon, Portugal. Could she dismiss the country's modest expectations for women, reminiscent of her earlier experience in Spain?

Part of interview in *High Fidelity:* The Artist's Life with Dorle J. Soria, April 1970
Elaine Shaffer begins a new career—she makes her podium debut. In Lisbon she will appear as conductor

and soloist in Vivaldi and Mozart flute concertos and
as conductor in the Schubert Fifth. *I never planned to
conduct but when I was asked I accepted. Many things
in my life happen without planning. There is a destiny
one must follow.*

The thrilling prospect of this new adventure warranted a rare, expensive
phone call to mother to discuss a re-do of the dress. First, the powder-blue
sleeveless concert dress must be transformed with no time to spare. Sleeves
to cover bare arms are added, each with little buttons at the narrow wrist.
The long back zipper must be hidden with small fabric-covered buttons
to the waist.

Hotel Ritz
Lisbon, Portugal
April 9, 1970

Dear Daddie Rex and Mother,

*I did something that I wasn't sure was possible—it
still amazes me, because it seemed like I was watching and
listening to someone else. It was all somewhat as a dream,
and I certainly <u>never</u> expected to be more than 'accepted' in
a country where women are held in low esteem. But from
the first rehearsal, the orchestra people were so nice, attentive
and enthusiastic, that they carried me along over 12 days I
worked with them.*

*Saturday there was tremendous excitement in the hall
and the orchestra really played with <u>soul</u>. The solo did
not suffer at all—in fact I didn't have much time to be
introspective about the playing. We did LeClaire, and the
Mozart D Major. At intermission, after the concertos, there
was already cheering and applause, and after the symphony
(Schubert's 5ᵗʰ) even more.*

*The director of the Emissora National, Mr. Prado, whose
idea it was to ask me, was in tears, as was his wife, who
is concertmaster of the orchestra. It was an atmosphere of
warmth and love on all sides and the music was like that.*

*Efi says he has never seen me so free and uninhibited as
when conducting. His attitude is marvelous. I don't know
<u>any</u> other conductor-husband who would have been so*

generous under those circumstances. We are playing together in Antwerp on April 23 and he says he is going to get a "headache" and have me substitute for him.

Roy Coelho, *Diaro de Noticias,* Lisbon, April 5, 1970
Once more a success for the Academy of Instrumentalists of the Emissora Nacional with a program that attracted a large audience. We were already acquainted with the notable flutist, due to her previous appearances here, in model interpretations with mellow, round agreeable sonority and authentic style. As an orchestra conductor Elaine Shaffer also conquered our orchestra and our public. She knew what to conduct and how to conduct it. This debut will pave the way for her as an orchestra conductor . . . in the principal musical centers of Europe and America.

Joao de Freitas, *Branco O Secolo,* Lisbon, 6 April 1970
We are told that this concert was an absolute debut as a conductor . . . we must say we have never known of a more conclusive beginning of a career. The real truth is that it would seem that Elaine Shaffer has never done anything else in her life but conduct. Everything integrated into a perfectly harmonious whole. Her success was complete and well-deserved, translated into applause and repeated bows.

Perplexing Pain

Savoy Hotel
London
Oct 23, 1970
Dear Daddie Rex and Mother,
London concert (Oct. 18) was very good—Hephzibah played divinely. We had about ¾ full hall and very enthusiastic audience. The most enthusiasm I've ever experienced in London.
We flew to Geneva after that for overnight and then I drove 6 hours to Ascona to play Tuesday with George Malcolm.

Beautiful church and marvelous acoustics, good audience and spiritual atmosphere. I am exhausted and wondering how I can do the American tour. [proposed for Jan. 1971]

The main problem was a pain in the back of the head, which came after 4 treatments by the therapist in London. He is so gentle, I don't know what he could have done wrong but since Saturday I had the pain. (Had to take pills in the middle of both concerts, because it becomes worse by blowing.) I will go to Berne earlier next week and see Prof. Hadorn.

Nov. 6, 1970

Dear Daddie Rex and Mother,

Since the London concert, Oct. 18, the pain in back of head got worse until a week ago I drove to Berne (with terrible pain) to Professor Hadorn—he injected something into the skull but it didn't help—drove back to Gstaad— there were about 48 hrs. almost unbearable. In Saanen they took x-rays. Prof. Hadorn gave strong pain-killers—couldn't practice more than a few hours in those 2 weeks but want to do the concert in Berne. Prof. Hadorn kept saying "you will play beautifully on Monday." Went to Berne for rehearsal and Hadorn gave 2 radium treatments. I stopped the medicine a day before the concert because it was making me dopey.

The anticipated Berne concert might have been overshadowed with the undiagnosed medical concerns. Instead Hephzibah and Elaine performed together on November 2, with Efrem conducting the Berne Symphony Orchestra, in a memorable all-Mozart concert.

4 November, 1970

It was a very special *concert—everyone said I never played better and some were in tears. The whole atmosphere was so warm and Efi was creating the whole thing. There were so many of our friends there: Wilmers, Alan Bennett (playwright and actor), Dr. and Mrs. Sollberger from Gstaad, the girl from the watch shop, Rosa, and others from Gstaad. Then, of course, Bishop and Mrs. Wertz (from Williamsport). Government heads of Switzerland were there. I said it was only because people were praying for me that I got through* that concert. *That kind of concert happens maybe once in ten years.*

Hephzibah had food poisoning all night and she also got a cold so Efi said he had 2 crippled soloists, but she played well too.

We decided to see Ormond-Clarke (London) and he took a long time with me. Says the disc is damaged from professional wear and tear of the flute playing. He says to rest for minimum 2 wks for ½ day each day and have hot compresses. No more radium. It is apparently between the 5th and 6th vertebrae, but the pain is mostly concentrated on the right side behind the ear.

Now we are glad Russia has postponed the tour. I hope this resting will do the trick—only feel OK when lying flat in bed. But do not take pills now and the pain is bearable.

Chalet El Camino
Gstaad
9 November 1970

Dear Mother and Daddie Rex,

My letter from London was anything but cheerful, and I want you to know that for the first time today I feel that there is a glimmer of hope that the pain will go away. Today we phoned Mrs. Wurmser about a rental and she mentioned her son is here from Basel. He is a brilliant neurologist in Basel hospital (36 yrs. old). We asked to see him. He seemed to understand my problem immediately and said the only thing that can help is an injection in the nerve and he found the spot right away. Already it is better. I was not convinced about Osmond-Clark's instructions to do nothing but lie down and have heat.

18 November 1970

Yesterday the new young local doctor came and showed me how to make hot compresses with towels—how Efi can make light massages and how to lie down. He didn't give any medicine—that's the kind of doctor I like. He agreed with Osmond-Clark's diagnosis and method of treatment. The neurologist wants to give another injection, but the trip to

Basel and back would have done more harm than good. Dr. Steiger says if the disc is "used up" this trouble may come and go when I work hard. I'm going to try practicing and will see right away if it makes the pain worse.

Chalet El Camino
3780 Gstaad
10 December 1970

Dear Daddie Rex & Mother,
    It has been a difficult time. I have been trying to get rid of the pain in the head through every possible method. Finally went to a new gynecologist in Lausanne, and she recommended a wonderful therapist in the hospital. She helped me even after the first treatment, so I have been driving every other day to Lausanne to her. Also taking B12 injections. It is better but still not 24 hours without pain. Practicing definitely brings pain, but it is bearable. Sir Henry Osmond-Clarke advised me to cancel the tour, but then he wanted Efi to give up conducting in 1955! I am not cancelling yet.

Gstaad
14 Dec. 1970

Dear Daddie Rex and Mother,
    Only to keep you posted—yesterday I drove to Basel to see Dr. Wurmser—he is such a darling. He said he would take me Sunday to have more time. He injected 4 needles in my head—then gave me the medicine to take along in case I need more injections, also some pills in case the pain gets worse when playing.
    After being with him an hour he asked me to his house for coffee with his wife—then I drove home—so much <u>traffic</u>, so it took 3¼ hrs. Going in the morning was only 2½ hrs.
    I called Toni Pieri, our friend in Florence, after having written him. He said the only thing that can help is to try the injections again. He is so smart—only by the letter he knew exactly what was wrong, even used the name of the nerve that the neurologist had used. And to think both of those boys are under 40.

Once Elaine determined to undertake a tour across the Atlantic with Hephzibah the perplexing maladies were hidden from her public. Response to her performances in her native country, in our hometown, and especially in New York City, assured a future reception on this continent.

New Courage
1971-73

The North American tour took Elaine and Hephzibah to Ottawa, Montreal, Boston, Charleston, West Virginia, New Orleans and Williamsport, Pennsylvania. It concluded in New York City with their recital in Alice Tully Hall at Lincoln Center. Reviews spoke of **'their performance styles (that) blend neatly to achieve interpretations of aristocratic sensitivity and quality. (Miss Shaffer's) flute playing is refined and subtle in its reflections, but it can be quite spirited, and . . . invariably alive in its phrasings. The tone was always smooth and beautifully controlled.'** Allen Hughes, *The New York Times*, Feb. 1, 1971

Elaine's hometown in Pennsylvania feted both musicians with enthusiastic ovations after their performance in Williamsport's Scottish Rite Auditorium. At intermission Lycoming College awarded Elaine an honorary doctorate degree in humanities. Lock Haven State College awarded her with the Commonwealth of Pennsylvania Department of Education Citation after her performance in their town. Local citizens followed her career from its early beginnings in their public schools and now boasted of her international acclaim.

Five years earlier "Elaine Shaffer Day" was declared by Williamsport Mayor Knaur on January 30, 1965, her first visit to her native state. Headlines and the oversized lettering on the marquee of the Capital Theater lighted Fourth Street. Ticket holders booked all 2300 seats and long lines extended around the block in anticipation of the concert. Some chose to stand rather than miss the event. The Harrisburg Symphony, under conductor Edwin McArthur, supported Elaine's Mozart *G Major Concerto*. A nostalgic and grateful public endeared her with tremendous applause and a standing ovation.

Return to Europe

Dear Mother,

Hoped to write from Belgium (Antwerp) but had unexpected rehearsal in afternoon and the morning I worked with Zabaleta alone. Next morning rehearsal and concert at night. We had fabulous success and felt in good form again. Concert was for the annual Gala of the Lions Club—everyone dressed and elegant. We were told they would probably not be very quiet and not applaud much. But the performance was so spellbinding they had to react and they really went crazy. Seven bows at the end. At the reception they were all so enthusiastic, like something had really happened. Was glad I had taken the light blue dress, otherwise would have been less dressed than they. Amazing what a week in Gstaad did—breathing was again effortless and I felt generally very strong.

The spring season imposed untimely stress over their imminent displacement from Le Pavillon. The owner made requests in unusual and bizarre messages and indicated her plan to reclaim her property. During Elaine's most demanding season Mrs. Harkness would, on short notice, send word of her intention to visit or occupy the chalet, and then not appear. Unreal expectations in dealing with the chalet unnerved Elaine. The Kurtz' belongings were carefully packed and labeled to prepare to move. *I have a notebook with every item written and every box and suitcase has a number.*

They explored farms, chateaus, apartments, and chalets. Some that showed *lots of money, but little taste.* Elaine had in mind the ideal site, off-road, convenient to airports, with trees, etc. and they came close to identifying it in one or two properties. Nothing was decided, fortunately, and an apartment, Chalet Mandi II, adjoining the Palace Hotel, was convenient. Elaine felt cozy in this manageable small apartment. Le Pavillon had been experienced as 'paradise' and now they must leave it.

I was reading <u>Narcissus and Goldmund</u> *by Herman Hesse, (a marvelous book), and one line was appropriate. He*

*had wandered many years and then came back to a place he
had once lived and worked. The man that he expected to see
was dead and his daughter was unfriendly to Goldmund—
he felt rejected. 'Suddenly street and city became transformed,
had the unfamiliar face that familiar things take on when
our heart has taken leave of them.' That is how I feel about
Pavillon.*

3789 Gstaad
9 April 1971

Dear Beverly,

*Our Zurich concert was very special . . . some used the
word miracle. Efi said I never played the Mozart G major
like that. I came out about 10 times after the concerto and
they applauded about 2 minutes before I even started to
play . . . it was the blue dress! I was aware of a strange but
very real sensation of being surrounded by several people, all
of whom have left this life, beginning with Mozart himself,
then Karl Barth, whose notes about Mozart were printed
in the program . . . I could only think about the "cloud of
witnesses." After such a concert one does not feel that one has
DONE something, but that one witnessed an event. It was
my debut in Zurich! There was an old professor who wouldn't
let me play, but he is retiring now . . . sooner or later they
die off.*

*This concert gave me a little courage to continue . . . after
feeling inadequate, and wondering whether NOW is the time
to retire, before I start playing too badly.*

*Dr. Boesch from Bircher-Benner wrote about my blood
test and prescribed medicine for anemia. He says it shows I am
over-tired and should have long rests between performances,
sleep a lot at night, etc. I knew that I was too tired, or run
down, and already suspected something was not quite OK.*

Elaine's musical career was at its pinnacle. In June there were concerts
in Dusseldorf before an audience of 2000. And in London, four strenuous
days of recording with Hephzibah.

Airmail letters in early 1972 bulged with glowing reviews, each critic
delving for poetic, ethereal language to describe unspeakable musical

experiences. Her concert schedule seemed impossible, even if she had been in excellent health. Between January 24 and April 3, there were concerts in Strasbourg, La Chaux de Fonds, Prague, East and West Berlin, San Remo, Madrid, Milan and Perugia. Each performance inevitably led to future engagements—nine concerts in East Berlin, Dresden, Leipzig, Jena—a two-week tour, plus two months in Socialist countries—Poland, Budapest, USSR, and two weeks of master classes, scheduled for August 1973 in Prague.

Gstaad
9 April 1972
Dear Mother and Dad,
Guess I told you about the breathing trouble I have had ever since the beginning of Jan. when we were doing packing in the cold cellar at Pavillon. Coughing all the time like a heavy smoker. Took a lot of cough medicines and saw doctors 3 times who said it is NOTHING. Yesterday it was worse so I went to Solberger and he wants to take an x-ray of the lungs. I am anemic (77% red cells) and low blood pressure (100/55). Gave injections of iron, and some pills, and today I don't feel that choking in the chest at all—amazing, so quickly. He is a good doctor, but I always hate to bother him when there are so many broken legs and operations. I was worrying about the concerts next week in Madrid. Have made an appointment with a great doctor in London for June 5th. Today we walked for 2 hours.

Salem Spital
Berne
April 18, 1972
First look at x-rays of lungs! *I would have tho't they belonged to someone else—a rather large spot on upper lung.*

The detailed letter addressed to each of her family members showed her sketch of the lung. She didn't hear Dr. Solberger call her name to look at the x-rays (distracted by a serious auto accident outside the window).

He wanted me to cancel Madrid, but then said I could go if I didn't do anything except rest and play the rehearsals and concerts.

In Madrid the sun was shining and it was a tonic just to be there. Our three concerts were the best ever (The Mozart Flute and Harp Concerto with Zabaleta and a German conductor, who was a very nice man, but musically not exactly my type). The house was full—3000 people each time and they screamed at the last note—we came out 6-7 times. Sunday morning audience was the greatest—they were like at a bull fight.

We flew to Geneva and I drove to Berne.

Next morning I came to Salem Hospital. They started with x-rays of lung, then blood, EKG etc. Prof. Hadorn is so wonderful, couldn't be more attentive—worked all day and evening on the x-rays and consultation with another doctor. Then he called Efi out and when they came back Efi was crying. So I know they are not keeping anything from me! There are no signs of cancer in the blood report. It could be a kind of virus, or TB and still a possibility of malignancy. He took me to another hospital and there a Prof. Senn, a fine surgeon, agreed the next step is to take out the little lump on the neck, and what ever result it shows would also apply to the lung. Have to cancel the two concerts in Italy. I don't feel bad, except for the usual breathing trouble, but it's been like that for almost 4 months. I am worried how Efi will hold up though—he doesn't want to eat and wants to cancel his concerts!

P. S. Everyone asked if I smoke! (Efi stopped smoking 15 years previously.)

Reason to Rejoice

After the treatment for inoperable lung cancer, Elaine selected the familiar Savoy Hotel and Middlesex Hospital in London, her preferred city and hospital, for the follow-up series of radiation treatments. Here she would celebrate spring, walk in its parks and attend select concerts. Mother and brother Bob arrived and brought the comfort of family to oversee her progress. Dad and Pat arrived later.

9 May 1972

Dear Daddie Rex,

Yesterday was the 2ⁿᵈ treatment and no side effects. Also saw Dr. Goldman, who has been my doctor for 20 yrs and he was sweet and reassuring. He measured my lung capacity and says I should be able to play flute—but not climb Everest!

14 July 1972

Dear Daddie Rex and Mother.

We have reason to rejoice. Dr. Jelliffe was pleased about my improved condition and on the phone said, "There is an enormous improvement in all three areas—I am extremely happy."

Chalet Mandi 2
3780 Gstaad
23 July 1972

Dear Mother & Daddie Rex,

Driving here I felt like the Jew going to Jerusalem. All of the familiar sights seemed somehow new. The air is something one almost forgets—the crispness and clarity of it. The atmosphere could not be more loving and pleasant. First night our landlords (Scherz) invited us upstairs for champagne. Then they brought sandwiches from the hotel and gave me a year pass for the swimming pool at the hotel.

Cooking has not been difficult. I made ratatouille one day—it was very good! Poppers, Wilmers, and Bigelows invited us for lunch. Everyone looks at me in the village with curiosity. They are waiting to see whether I will really play on August 22. There are rumors that this will be the last Festival and that Yehudi wants to sell his house.

I have practiced every day and Efi is working on his orchestra parts for the concerts in Zurich in October. The first days breathing was difficult, but is improving. We are walking a bit each day. There is still that pressure on the neck, more in the evenings. Dr. Jelliffe said it could go a long time like that.

Elaine called it one of those perfect days when she welcomed John Solum, and his wife Penny. She took them and their two boys to Turbach to walk and picnic.

The boys (5 and 8 yrs.) were delighted to be able to play in the creek, etc. We walked about an hour each way. I'm glad they are here. [John and Elaine performed together at the Gstaad Festival August 22nd.]

Sunday Aug. 6, 1972

Dear Mother,

John and I have already rehearsed together twice and it is a pleasure to play with him. At least we will be prepared if no one else at this festival is—two concertos in one evening, but not too difficult.

Next Tuesday 15th, I intend to drive (with Efi) to Zurich for rehearsal with the Zurich Chamber Orchestra and then the 18th we go to Bludenz (Austria) 2 hrs. drive from Zurich, for the concert. There I am playing a concerto that I've never done before but have been working on for 3 years.

Right now it's so peaceful and beautiful looking out on the garden, the mountains. It's like those September days that you know. August 1st National Holiday, it was cloudy during the day but mysteriously cleared in the eve for fires on all the mountain tops. Then at 10 PM the Palace Hotel had their own fireworks which was like having them in our garden.

Of course, all of these things have an added meaning to me, remembering 3 months ago, and not knowing whether I would see it again, not to mention being able to walk.

Geneva airport
Sunday August 27, 1972

Dear Daddie Rex, Mother and Pat,

Coming from London and taking a plane to Nice. I was rather exhausted after the rehearsal, concerts and trips. Dr. Jelliffe took 3 x-rays and said there was additional improvement—said "we are going in the right direction." He heard what I had done in the last week and said, "you are acting like a teenager."

Today (in London) we visited Solomon and his wife, the greatest English pianist who had a stroke in 1956. He asked about Bob—remembered him from St. Moritz when he played there. It made us sad to see him—they are both extraordinary people and real friends.

Dr. Jelliffe thinks the swelling at the neck and pain in chest and back is caused by the strain of playing. I do not intend to practice for a week in Antibes. It is hard to stop after getting "in form."

London—end of Sept for check-up, also Oct. 15th for Bach concert Oct. 22nd

Aarhus (Denmark)—Oct. 27 to play the 30th with orchestra

Copenhagen—Oct. 31st recital with Hephzibah

The mention of a week's reprieve seemed hardly enough to meet such demands.

The Height of Musical Powers

The October concert in London's Queen Elizabeth Hall was considered a daunting feat for a robust woodwind artist. Elaine would be playing six Bach *Flute Sonatas* from memory and only those closest to her knew she was in remission from inoperable lung cancer. Perhaps this undertaking had been her dream, or was it personally conceived soon after the reality of her diagnosis?

> *It may sound crazy to do such a thing, but it is something to work on. It is 79 minutes without the repeats.*

The performance of October 22, 1972 was on her 47th birthday.

> *It seems everyone felt the uniqueness of the occasion, even those not aware of our 'secret.'*
>
> *I can only say it was another blessing, almost a miracle. Even with a 2 hr. concert no one felt its length. No one got up to leave at the end.*
>
> *Am sending the program with John's (Solum) interesting program notes. We found the lithograph of Bach's portrait in Berne, and his signature in Albert Schweitzer's book on Bach. (John reconstructed one of the movements Bach left uncompleted.)*
>
> *Dr. Goldman was so pleased about the concert. He said, "Ironically you are right now at the height of your musical powers. Because you have seen the depths—nothing can happen to you—there is no more struggle. Not many people can have that experience." He is sometimes tremendously perceptive. I really felt that there were waves of thoughts*

coming through on that evening. A certain calm was there that was supernatural.

Chalet Mandi
7 Nov. 1972

Dear Paola,

The great test and my big satisfaction is the London concert on my birthday—all the Bach Sonatas with George Malcolm. It was a wonderful evening—one of those where I felt privileged to be there as a sort of "medium" to let the music come through. It did not seem an effort to me, though it lasted 2 hrs and Bach is the most difficult thing for breathing there is. The hall was sold out 2 days before and they turned away 100 people at the door. Dr. Jelliffe (radiologist) was there—very happy as you can imagine.

Stoddard Lincoln, *The Financial Times,* London, Oct. 23, 1972

Last night's concert of six sonatas for flute and harpsichord was a sheer delight . . . the evening offered a richness in variety which the printed programme did not suggest.

Elaine Shaffer is one of the most elegant performers gracing the stage today . . . her entire body expresses the music. Phrasing and dynamic blend with gesture and stance to create a beautiful unity. Even in the most difficult passage work she is able to bring out a sequential structure with echoes or bring to it a sense of urgency or, where required, humour. To hear Miss Shaffer's Bach is to hear it at its best . . . a superb reading of this wonderful work terminated the evening in a blaze of glory.

Critics from the (London) Times and Telegraph did not come, disgraceful since it was never done before and not again very soon.

Time magazine on several occasions chose Elaine for a feature story, only to displace her with another choice. The Bach Sonatas from memory with solo flute had never been done. Elaine intimated that the London performance was newsworthy. Instead, the January 1 Music Page of *Time* featured Elaine with Aaron Copland, her premier, and their recording of his composition, *Duo for Flute and Piano*.

> *Time*, January 1, 1973
> **Just as there was no doubt that the man to write the piece should be Aaron Copland, so there was no doubt that the flutist to play it should be Elaine Shaffer.**
>
> **Shaffer had learned virtually everything she knew about the flute from Kincaid. Shortly before his death in 1967 at the age of 71, he had handed down his extraordinary platinum flute for her. She was not just the queen of the flute, but one of the world's two or three finest concert flutists, male or female. In 1971 Shaffer and Hephzibah Menuhin gave the world première of the new work at a benefit for Philadelphia's Settlement Music School, with Copland in attendance. Last week in New York, Shaffer recorded the work for Columbia Records, this time with Copland, 72, at the piano.**

During the recording interlude in New York, our family visited Elaine at The Anchorage, summer home of Efrem's sister and brother-in-law the William Rosenwalds. I found it a precious time to catch-up on news, walk the expansive grounds on Long Island Sound, and enjoy a game of table tennis at her suggestion. A broad smile of amusement radiated: *"Do you know where I go here to have my treatment monitored? The coroner's office in Port Chester!"* We do not say goodbye. Already, in better times, especially during my visit in 1968 in London and Gstaad, we had talked easily at length about suffering, life's meaning and divine purpose.

Each time I am with her she is more than I remembered. Elaine wrote this of her friend, Hephzibah. Yes, the words speak for me when I recall my last visit with Elaine!

"Get the latest Time magazine—the Man of the Year issue!" This phone call alerted me to the magazine coverage of Elaine and the Copland

recording. The return flight to Europe was delayed as she gathered up copies of *Time* magazine, January 1, 1972. Friends who gathered at the airport for her farewell painted a hopeful picture of Elaine mounting the steps of the airliner, weighed down with a bundle of magazines!

The Middlesex Hospital

An extensive letter in cramped handwriting, written from her London Hospital bed, was dated January 22, 1973, the day she was scheduled to perform in Germany.

> *Dear Mother,*
>
> *Only want you to know things are going pretty well. For 3 days now temperature is normal, breathing better, coughing less. I am hoping Dr. Jelliffe will agree to my trying to get out of bed for the 1ˢᵗ time tomorrow, at least for a few minutes. He expects the lung to clear up, with treatments, and that I can play again.*
>
> *Efi has such a hard schedule in the next weeks, but it's a good thing he went away. He was in a terrible state when he left, but from Geneva, since he is working, he sounds like a different person. Tomorrow night is the concert in Germany—they are not having <u>any</u> soloist in my place.*
>
> *You know that I think of all of you, and send all my love. Please excuse the scribble—never could write in bed!*
>
>

Middlesex Hospital
Woolavington Wing
Sunday January 28

>
> *Dearest Beverly*
>
> *Will probably be here until Feb. 22, as Dr. Jelliffe is continuing treatments two more weeks. The treatments have been causing nausea the last 3 days and the difficulty in swallowing has also started. But one can stand it if the results will be good.*
>
> *Vera Courts brings me salad and washes the nightgowns. Mrs. Baer brings chicken soup twice a week. John and Penny Solum come <u>every</u> day. Today Richard Hauser is coming— Hephzibah is in America. Efi calls at least 3 times a day, now*

in Brussels. I heard his concert from Geneva on the radio! It was very exciting!

Sorry this is such a selfish letter, but I want to tell you the details, which may have got distorted or just overlooked in the relaying process. Am running out of steam and paper. No one should worry when I don't write. If there is something urgent I would phone you.

Much love to you & Aaron and children,

Some of Elaine's last words were scribbled on the pale blue sheets of Savoy Hotel stationery.

Death is stronger than life,
But love is stronger than death. Kahil Gilbran

Don't ask "why me" when didn't ask before.

Every one of us is the same—the only difference is the inevitable that our distance from (?) has changed.

Vacation-perfection-extended a few more days-but departure still must be faced—last day more intense than the first.

After skiing accident-usual remark—'I had 15 years of good fun'—life has been good—loving, being loved, being free. Enjoying the gifts and sharing them.

Mountains to Grubenberg—darkness, then a new vista—new level of existence.

Last trill of Mozart Flute and Harp Concerto with great crescendo—never played like that before and not indicated in the score.

Three most important things. Love Be Loved Be Free. No sadness without joy—no joy without sadness. Always a mixture.

Elaine died in London's Middlesex Hospital on 19 February 1973.

A Tribute

Delivered at a celebration of the life of Elaine Shaffer, The First Presbyterian Church, Philadelphia, PA, 23 Feb. 1973 by The Rev. Robert W. Shaffer

In the novel *Jean-Christophe* Romain Rolland wrote: "Most men die at twenty or thirty; thereafter they are only reflections of themselves: for the rest of their lives they are aping themselves, repeating from day to day more and more mechanically and affectedly what they said and did and thought and loved when they were alive."

While it may be true for many, it was not true for the one whose life we celebrate. Because she truly lived while she was alive, she is not dead though she died. In a deep sense she lives and continues this day to call us into more and more life.

<u>Elaine loved life</u>, physical life with its insights, sounds, smells, sensation of touch, strenuous work and play. She invites us who have stopped loving these good bodies of ours to take them for walks
on quiet beaches, or
      mountain trails, or
           early morning streets;
to permit our eyes to stop and ponder the face of an old person or
      a little child;
to permit our sense of smell to embrace wood fire,
      wild flowers, and
           baking bread.

<u>Elaine loved people</u>. She was sensitive to the needs of others. When touched by the inclination to
      make a call,

write a letter, or
send a gift,
she did not procrastinate.
And the word, the gift and the moment always seemed right.
So too she calls us to be sensitive to those delicate signals
which others send out
to be heard only by those who really care:
to speak those words of love to others which
unspoken
are carried quickly away
like twigs on a mountain stream.

Elaine was inexpressibly courageous.
Whether seen as a young teen-age girl without formal training going to
audition before the renowned William Kincaid; or leaving the security of
posts with established American orchestras to go to another continent to
do what no other woman flutist had ever done; or, last spring facing the
fact that she had cancer, setting her face peacefully without self-pity, to go
on to give the world some of her greatest performances.
Like the sound of a thousand trumpets,
her life proclaimed
there is nothing which can happen to us
which can conquer life
except
our refusal to live it.

Elaine loved excellence, something more than perfection.
Where perfection can be achieved by a machine-like performer,
it must be wedded to a passionate human spirit
to give birth to excellence.
It was for this reason she loved Bach.
Bach joined supreme inspiration with the discipline of unsurpassed artistry
and beauty was born of which we never tire.
Herman Hesse expressed it in Narcissus and Goldmund:
"to him art and craftsman were worthless unless
they burned like the sun and
had the power of storms.
He had no use for anything that brought only comfort,
pleasantness,

only small joys.
He was searching for other things."
And so was she.

She calls us today to commit ourselves to that suffering necessary to give
shape to those works of music and art and words
known to us now only as intimations and deep longings;
to understand the brevity of life and
its unrepeated opportunities.

Elaine loved God.
Not the god who can be captured, known with familiarity, systemized,
and kept in special buildings,
but the gracious source of all life and being,
ranging free like the wind,
unconditionally for all.
Because she, like Bach, drew life from its wellspring
she played his music with such empathy and beauty
her listeners often found themselves with tears.

She told of times during performances when she felt herself
transported,
carried up out of herself,
as if her whole being was an instrument
picked up in the hands of the master and
played with exquisite joy.
So too she calls us to return to our roots,
to our beginnings,
to our visions of what we once felt
we could be
and
in this world

When a person of such infinite worth dies,
sooner
or
later
if we are to live as she lives
we must forgive death

and so escape the mastery of its shadow.

Death is forgiven
the moment we are able to lift our heads again
and behold a future
                          enticing us and daring us to seize it
and make it yield its potential for good.

At that moment we join Elaine in her victory over death.

CPSIA information can be obtained at www.ICGtesting.com
Printed in the USA
BVOW020055041211

277374BV00004B/5/P